What people are saying about Michael Harris

In *Welcome to the Rebellion,* Harris explains how George Lucas' modern myth is rooted in radical political resistance against corporate authoritarianism with a message more relevant today than in the 1970s when it was conceived. He reveals the underlying political message of the *Star Wars* saga and its radical message which makes it more than a popcorn film, it's a document for resistance.
Jason Ward – Owner and Editor-in-chief of MakingStarWars.net

For all of us who love *Star Wars,* for all of us who love humanity and our planet, for all of us who yearn to be part of the Rebel Alliance, this book is for you. Harris has given us this incredible resource to study *Star Wars,* so that we can learn the ways of the Force, understand the very real and violent Empire of structural inequality and systems of supremacy we are up against today, and learn about the values and commitments of the also very real Rebel Alliance. Get this book, full of brilliant lessons and insights, study it, share it with others, and let it help us be the Rebels and Jedis for collective liberation that the world so desperately needs.
Chris Crass – Author of *Towards Collective Liberation* and *Towards the "Other America",* social justice educator and member of the Rebel Alliance

Also by Michael Harris

Welcome to the Rebellion, Zero Books, ISBN: 978-1-78904-367-9

Stay Alive

Surviving Capitalism's Coming Hunger Games

Stay Alive

Surviving Capitalism's Coming Hunger Games

Michael Harris

zer0 books

Winchester, UK
Washington, USA

JOHN HUNT PUBLISHING

First published by Zero Books, 2021
Zero Books is an imprint of John Hunt Publishing Ltd., No. 3 East St., Alresford,
Hampshire SO24 9EE, UK
office@jhpbooks.com
www.johnhuntpublishing.com
www.zero-books.net

For distributor details and how to order please visit the 'Ordering' section on our website.

ISBN: 978 1 78904 611 3
978 1 78904 612 0 (ebook)
Library of Congress Control Number: 2020933687

A CIP catalogue record for this book is available from the British Library.

Design: Stuart Davies

UK: Printed and bound by CPI Group (UK) Ltd, Croydon, CR0 4YY
Printed in North America by CPI GPS partners

Contents

Previous titles by the author

A Future for Planning: Taking Responsibility for Twenty-First Century Challenges (Abingdon: Routledge, 2019). ISBN: 9781138708808

Welcome to the Rebellion: A New Hope In Radical Politics (Winchester: Zero Books, 2020). ISBN: 9781789043679

Disclaimer

Neither this book nor its contents are endorsed or approved by or affiliated in any way with Suzanne Collins, Scholastic, Lionsgate or any of their representatives. The opinions contained herein are those of the author only. *The Hunger Games* and related terms are the registered trademarks of District 12, LLC and Lions Gate Entertainment Inc.

Preface: "If we burn, you burn with us"

In July 2019, a new theme park opened in the People's Republic of China. Located in Hengqin, Zhuhai, in the Guangdong-Hong Kong-Macau Greater Bay Area, Lionsgate Entertainment World is a movie-themed "vertical theme park" spanning 22,000 square meters of indoor space. Designed to appeal to the "young adult dating crowd," it features attractions based on franchises owned by the major American media corporation. These include *The Hunger Games*, Suzanne Collins' hugely successful future dystopian fiction series about a totalitarian regime and its annual state-sanctioned child murder pageant.

As described by *Forbes* magazine, "With an entire level devoted to *The Hunger Games,* visitors will be immersed in the wealthy Capitol City with a gold and marble streetscape, a themed gourmet restaurant, a bakery, and a hair salon inspired by the outrageous styles in the film." Inadvertently echoing the desperate enthusiasm of Effie Trinkett (a character from the series), Selena Magill, General Manager of Lionsgate Entertainment World, exclaimed that: "We expect guests in China and all around the world to enjoy sensational experiences here that they won't soon forget."

For a more authentic experience, fans could travel just an hour away to Hong Kong, where the Beijing-backed government was clamping down on the protest movement led by young people against very real encroaching Chinese tyranny. At times the streets of the city resembled scenes from the films, with Hong Kong police, acting like *The Hunger Games'* perversely named Peacekeepers (state military police), beating young people in the streets and firing tear gas indiscriminately into crowds, while protesters brandished bows and fire-dipped arrows.

The loosely coordinated but often highly disciplined protesters, drawn from the self-described "cursed generation," used social media savvily, often employing tropes from popular culture, including spray painting one familiar (to *Hunger Games'* fans) slogan on walls and subways: "If we burn, you burn with us." The protesters wore black, like the forces of the Mockingjay revolution (the rebellion in *The Hunger Games*), while pro-government agents and Triad thugs wore white, like President Snow (the dictator of the series' fictional country of Panem) and his brutal army of Peacekeepers.

This wasn't the first time protesters had drawn on the series. In 2014, during the Umbrella Revolution, they'd used the three-finger salute from the story, a symbol of solidarity and defiance. After the failure of their first rebellion, the protesters left signs reading "We'll be back."

They kept their promise. The year 2019 saw months of sustained protests and mass marches. But the Hong Kong and international business community largely looked on, while investors only fretted about the impact on China's plans to turn the region into a financial and technological hub to rival Silicon Valley – a gleaming twenty-first century Capitol (the wealthy ruling city of Panem), surrounded by servile industrial districts and factories with "suicide nets" to stop workers killing themselves.

The protests were for freedom and democracy, a last chance for basic rights. But they also represented anger at Hong Kong's largely unregulated capitalism, with young people priced out of the most expensive housing market in the world and seeing few opportunities in their future, all the while being ordered to act as "patriotic citizens" by the super-wealthy political-business elite who run the city.

An uber-rich ruling class gorge themselves in a futuristic playground, while working people struggle to survive in exploited rural areas. The possibility of revolution is only a distant memory, a forgotten hope kept at bay by brutal policing, aching poverty and a rigidly segregated class system. *The*

Hunger Games could be seen as a critique of states like China – an authoritarian, propagandized, militarized, state capitalist economy, which runs prison camps for political dissidents, including using forced labor to supply goods for Western corporations. But that wasn't the series' aim. Its setting is a post-collapse North America. It's both a warning about the near future and a cutting critique of the present-day United States, of reality TV politics, the demonization of the poor, state violence and oligarchy.

When *The Hunger Games* began in 2008 – it's since become a defining story for a generation that's grown up with economic crisis and never ending war – many commentators lumped it in with other young adult genre fiction such as *Twilight* and *Divergent*. But *The Hunger Games* is political. It's about an elder elite that uses state power, a compliant media and violent spectacle to pacify its population. It's about how a rebellion is sparked by defiance and spreads through subversive symbols, while the regime responds in the only way it knows.

The year 2019 saw youth-led revolts in other countries as well, from Chile to Lebanon, Thailand to Columbia. Despite different local flashpoints, underlying all of them were extreme inequalities which especially disadvantage young people, and the willingness of elites to crush any challenges to their power. The world hadn't seen a wave of street protests like this since the late 1980s, surpassing the scale of the Arab Spring protests of the early 2010s.

In an important sense, *The Hunger Games* predicts how regimes around the world are likely to respond to increasing youth-led protests against their power. It's about collapse, war, rebellion, trauma and recovery. It's dark, emotionally and politically truthful, and while it doesn't flinch from the horrors of its setting, it's also ultimately, eventually, realistically hopeful. It's a story about how regimes fall, but how the revolution against power and exploitation can never end. And with the climate crisis and environmental disaster, it's about a coming future of enforced scarcity and segregation, and an emerging form of authoritarian statism we'll call capitolism. It's the story of our times, and most likely of our future as well.

The real hunger games are just beginning. We need to return to Panem.

Introduction: "Real or not real?"

"There must be some special girl. Come on, what's her name?"

The first book in the series, *The Hunger Games*, introduces us to Panem through Katniss Everdeen, a 16-year-old woman. In just a few pages, we learn about the world she wakes up in everyday. We enter the deprived, slave labor prison of District 12, where most people don't have enough food to eat, and the Seam, the dirt poor coal-mining area where Katniss lives with her mother and her younger sister Prim.

Katniss has lost her father in a mine explosion a few years before. We're given a sense of her psychological damage from poverty and loss. Katniss's mother is "blank and unreachable" after her husband's death. Katniss is in many ways also numb to the world. She's annoyed at her mother for shutting down, but she doesn't really see how she's done the same.

Katniss is a survivor, practically in using her hunting skills to secure a little more food for her family, and emotionally in finding her own ways to cope. Given the knowledge she's inherited from her father, Katniss could provide for her family, but hunting is illegal.

The Hunger Games isn't just the brutally honest name of the annual fight-to-the-death competition organized by the Capitol, the city that dominates Panem. It's the way that its elite controls the districts. Starvation, scarcity and minimal rewards doled out to subservient districts; the Capitol uses hunger as a weapon against the masses. It's also a powerful metaphor for the economic system we live under today, so much so that "the Hunger Games" has now become shorthand for any especially brutally competitive environment or economy.

Despite this, Katniss is a natural rebel, though she doesn't think of herself that way (in time she will, though). She finds the weak spots in the fence surrounding the district and escapes into the woods to hunt, but really just to find a few hours of freedom in her highly-surveilled society. And yet, Katniss' acts of everyday rebellion will have major consequences. They will come to represent the seeds of a different world.

"It's to the Capitol's advantage to have us divided among ourselves"

Like all of Panem's subjects, Katniss has learned it's not safe to criticize the system. She's somewhat aware of the impact this has had on her, to "hold my tongue and to turn my features into an indifferent mask so that no one could ever read my thoughts." Looming over her, over all of the young people who live in the districts, is the Hunger Games, a brutal televised fight to the death. Today is reaping day, the day of the public lottery for participation in the Games.

The odds that any given child will be selected for the Games are relatively low, lower in districts with large populations (unlike the small District 12). But the fear is real. Even here, the Capitol reinforces its control through division. Another reason why District 12 is looked down on is that it's only produced two winners of the Games in the previous 73 years, including the perpetually drunk mentor Haymitch Abernathy (former victors in the Games are forced to become mentors to the competitors, called "tributes," from their districts). Other districts, those more favored by the Capitol, are better trained to compete. Their tributes, called "careers," even look forward to being chosen for the Games.

The Seam, where Katniss lives in District 12, is the poorest of the poor. But some families in District 12 are comparatively better off, for example those who run small businesses. They can reduce the likelihood that their children will be selected for the Games, whereas the likes of Katniss and her closest friend Gale are forced through threat of starvation to increase their odds of selection in exchange for desperately needed food rations. As Gale says, it's the Capitol's strategy to divide the districts between each other, and within them.

"You sit on a throne of lies"

The film of *The Hunger Games* starts differently from the book. After some introductory text, we open on a discussion between Caesar Flickerman, the Capitol's television host for the Games, and Seneca Crane, the Head Gamemaker who designs the Game arena. They're discussing the "bonding importance" of the Games, how it's "our tradition...the way we've been able to heal." At first the Games were a reminder of the first rebellion and the "price the districts had to pay," as enshrined in the country's Treaty of Treason, but now apparently it's "something that knits us all together."

The Capitol audience, comfortable in their plush auditorium, applauds warmly. Caesar asks Seneca what describes his "personal signature" as Gamemaker. Cut to a horrifying scream and a bleak shot of District 12. It's Prim, waking up on the day of the reaping after a nightmare. What defines the Games, this year and every year, is not healing, but horror.

The story in the books is told only from Katniss' point of view. This new scene added for the film emphasizes the political nature of the story, starting in the Capitol's construction of a self-justifying national myth, its attempt to rationalize oppression and exploitation in the name of order and unity. But what we mostly see is how the system affects the young people existing in the shadow of the Games, the horror they experience in the arena, and the psychological trauma of trying to survive under the Capitol's rule.

"Well, that's a sunny view of our situation"

Later, during the reaping ceremony (in the film version), a propaganda video is shown to the districts. President Snow, the ruler of Panem, provides the voice over, reiterating the "hard fought, sorely won" peace that his new order has ensured. But the video skips over the backstory mentioned in the book, of the environmental disasters that sparked the first rebellion decades before. Of course, this is only how the Capitol wants the districts to remember "our history."

The Hunger Games takes place at an unspecified future date, in the dystopian, post-apocalyptic nation of Panem, located in what is now the United States. The country is smaller than today, geographically and demographically. Large areas of land were made uninhabitable by rising sea levels and many people died (for example, the population of District 12 is said to be just 8000 people).

Panem consists of the wealthy ruling Capitol city, located in the Rocky Mountains, surrounded by 12 (originally 13) poorer districts. Katniss' District 12 is located in today's Appalachia. The furthest from the Capitol, it specializes in coal mining. District 13 was a center of military-industrial production. When the Capitol crushed the rebellion, it reduced District 13 to ashes.

The government is a dictatorship, a surveillance state in which the districts are forced into subservience to the Capitol, expected to provide goods in exchange for "protection," for peace and prosperity. But only the Capitol is lavishly rich and technologically advanced, while the districts survive in poverty and distress. In place of the actual history of America/Panem, the Hunger Games is part of a national myth, told by self-serving elites.

This myth contains a threat, to never risk returning to war, to the dark days of division. Conflict and the question of what makes a "just war" and a just revolution is a key question in the story. Panem's myth is a defense against revolution, in spite of (or because of) the terrible conditions experienced by most of its subjects. But as we come to learn, the state is war, the source of all violence.

"These things happen in war"

Panem is founded on a core consevative idea, one that still holds a powerful grip on today's politics: that the state restrains us from all-out civil war. This was first set out by the English philosopher Thomas Hobbes (1588-1679), particularly in his most famous book *Leviathan* (1651). Hobbes was informed by the English Civil War or civil wars of 1642-46 and 1648-51 – he often uses the word "rebellion" – that led to the execution of the king and the declaration of a republic.

At the time, England was divided, politically, economically, socially, religiously, then militarily. This was also an age of radical new movements, for example the Levellers called for much greater equality in wealth and political rights, while the Diggers fought for the abolition of wage labor. But these flourishing demands for justice and democracy were exactly what Hobbes warned against.

His argument was rooted in a deeply pessimistic view of human behavior, dressed up in some crude "science" (as conservatives still do today). We are driven by greed and fear. Without an authoritarian state, we compete, often violently, to secure the necessities of life and seek reputation ("glory"), both for its own sake and for greater security. Hobbes' state of nature is perpetual strife, endless dark days comprising a "war of all against all," leavened only by temporary alliances to stave off graver threats and imminent perils. Hobbes thought that the inevitable condition of humankind was one in which life is "solitary, poor, nasty, brutish, and short," a relentless quest for power that "ceaseth only in death."

In such bleakness, there is no alternative to strong central government. Even limiting its powers to seize the goods of its subjects without their consent undermines it. Our only "hope" is all-powerful authority. People must surrender their power to the ultimate peacekeeper, the sovereign ruler. But in reality, this idea just normalizes the actions of some selfish, amoral people as "natural," and supports exploitation and right-wing authoritarianism, even fascism.

"I'm sick of people lying to me for my own good"

There's a deeper, psychological explanation for this attachment to authoritarianism.

One of the thinkers we'll refer to in this book is Alice Miller, a Polish-Swiss psychologist/psychoanalyst noted for her work on parental child abuse, sometimes called "controversial" because she was so direct in her challenge to abuse and its links to authoritarianism.

In 1980, after having worked as a psychoanalyst for 20 years, Miller stopped practicing and teaching to explore childhood more systematically. She became critical of both Sigmund Freud and Carl Jung. By the time her fourth book was published, Miller no longer believed that psychoanalysis was viable. She later wrote about her time as a psychoanalyst that, "For twenty years I observed people denying their childhood traumas, idealizing their parents and resisting the truth about their childhood by any means." The question why would be the focus of Miller's most well-known books.

In *For Your Own Good* (1980), Miller introduced the concept of "poisonous pedagogy" to describe the child-rearing practices prevalent in Europe, especially before the Second World War. She believed that the pain inflicted on children "for their own good" was parents unconsciously re-enacting the trauma inflicted on them when they were children, continuing the cycle of trauma down generations.

Breaking Down the Wall of Silence (1990) is perhaps Miller's most explicitly political book. Written in the aftermath of the fall of the Berlin Wall, Miller takes to task the entirety of human culture. The "wall" is the metaphorical barrier behind which society (academia, psychiatrists, clergy, politicians and the media) seeks to protect itself by denying the mind-destroying effects of child abuse. Historically, children were seen as less than human, as evil wretches in need of constant coercion and control. The goal of child-rearing was to stamp out willfulness in children, to crush their spontaneity and spirit, thought necessary in order to make them upstanding and virtuous citizens.

To Miller, the command to "honor your parents" leads us to accept and repeat abusive parenting and direct our unresolved trauma either against others (through war, terrorism, delinquency) or ourselves (in eating disorders, drug addiction, depression). We use children as scapegoats for our past suffering. This is also the root of political authoritarianism: dictators seek to pass on their trauma to society, and we accept their abuses of power because of our indoctrination into the legitimacy of the harsh parent. Only by becoming aware of this can we break the chain of violence.

In *The Hunger Games*, the Capitol claims the right, the necessity, to rule over the otherwise disobedient citizens of Panem. The Games are for their own good. Panem needs to punish its children to avoid further conflict. Trauma is passed down and legitimized. And Katniss, like her peers, is emotionally numb and politically passive, despite her repressed rage at the cruelty of the Capitol. As Miller wrote in *Breaking Down the Wall of Silence*, "The reality of adult cruelty is so beyond their comprehension that the child is in a state of constant denial in order to survive."

Miller didn't accept that we're naturally evil. If we recognize the causes of trauma and the roots of authoritarianism, we can heal and recover. This is the emotional journey that Katniss will go on, and perhaps the one we all need to undertake.

"And they say no one ever wins the Games"

Far from being natural or necessary, this fundamentally authoritarian vision is as constructed as Panem, with its regimented districts and brutally competitive "reality" TV show. A much more benign view of how we can and do act can lead us to envisage a very different kind of society, in which centralizing power is not the solution, it's the problem. If this is the political journey that Katniss will go on, in another way, as we'll see, she was there from the beginning.

Another purpose of Hobbesian propaganda is that people will accept shortages, hardship, cruelty, misery and the curtailing of their freedom if you convince them they're in a perpetual state of war, or would be without the powerful parental state. As we'll see, even though many people in the districts don't fall for it, this ideology helps to justify their privation.

Of course, not all of our societies suffer under authoritarian regimes, despite Hobbesian thinking still being prevalent. But environmental, economic and political collapse, and the fear and chaos they will bring – our coming hunger games – are likely to lead us toward our own version of Panem.

"No, I want you to rethink it and come up with the right opinion"

The Hunger Games starts with a Hobbesian state, but never accepts it. This is based on a fundamentally different view of human nature to the Hobbesians. Not a naive view – Collins depicts the cruelty that people can inflict on others under an authoritarian ideology. But a view that suggests how the state is the real source of violence in society and how it engineers conflict as a means of control.

The alternative view is that our environment shapes how we behave, that left to our own devices we are more likely to find ways to cooperate peacefully, even to sacrifice ourselves for others, than we are to engage in an endless war against all. What raises *The Hunger Games* above most dystopian stories is that it also depicts how goodness can flourish even in the most dehumanizing circumstances.

It's possible to imagine a peaceful Panem without the state, a society of mutual trade and cooperation, of solidarity and fraternity, where people aren't defined by one means of livelihood but have the freedom to follow personal pursuits, to fish in the morning and do critical theory at night, without ever becoming a fisherman or a critic, as Karl Marx once said.

But Katniss can't allow herself to imagine this world for more than a moment, not because it would be against nature, but because the state would punish them harshly for even trying to live differently. She might be a survivor, but she's mired in resignation. Before the reaping, Katniss listens to Gale's dreams of escape, but can only respond that it's impossible, to leave their families, to put them at risk, let alone to hope that another Panem is possible.

"What am I supposed to do? Sit here and watch you die?"

Some dystopias drop us into howling post-collapse wastelands in which the problem is the lack of government, a lack of any institutions really, or travel through lawless cyberpunk cityscapes in which there's a lack of a state standing up to towering corporations. Hobbes would surely recognize his state of nature in these stories.

But *The Hunger Games* returns to an earlier dystopianism of state cruelty and coercion, of *Nineteen Eighty-Four* (one of Collins' favorite books), *Brave New World* and *Fahrenheit 451*. Some commentators take this to mean that the series is a right-wing libertarian treatise, but as we'll argue, this doesn't hold up. Collins never forgets who the real enemy is.

These themes are taken further in *The Ballad of Songbirds and Snakes*, Suzanne Collins' prequel to *The Hunger Games* trilogy, which takes place on the morning of the reaping of the 10th Games. As Collins says, "With this book, I wanted to explore the state of nature, who we are, and what we perceive is required for our survival...The reconstruction period 10 years after the war, commonly referred to as the Dark Days – as the country of Panem struggles back to its feet – provides fertile ground for characters to grapple with these questions and thereby define their views of humanity."

As we'll see, these views of human nature are also fundamentally about capitalism. The rationale for the Hobbesian state is also used by conservatives to justify an exploitative economic system in which elites dominate and the poor suffer. It's just as much a lie as Panem's propaganda is for punishing its districts.

But for now, the Capitol is in control. And it's Katniss' sister Prim, in her first reaping, who's selected for the Games.

"I volunteer!" I gasp. "I volunteer as tribute!"

When Katniss volunteers for the Games in place of her sister, the crowd understands it's suicide, given her district's poor record in the Games and its disadvantages against the other districts. Despite the Games supposedly being a national pageant, they respond with "the boldest form of dissent they can manage. Silence. Which says we do not agree. We do not condone." Despite the Capitol's relentless rationales for its exploitation and cruelty, its propaganda doesn't seem to be working. Later on, Katniss will learn that many other districts are also ready to defy the Capitol.

Although she doesn't intend it, Katniss' instinctive reaction to volunteer represents the start of a revolution, a spark that will ignite a fire that will eventually engulf Panem. What that revolution means, and what she's really fighting for, are critical questions at the heart of *The Hunger Games*.

"She has no idea, the effect that she can have"

And then, something unexpected happens. Almost every member of the crowd touches the three middle fingers of their left hand to their lips and holds them out to Katniss. It's an old, rarely used gesture in District 12. It means a combination of thanks, admiration and goodbye to a loved one.

The Hunger Games struck a chord from the start. Suzanne Collins established her name in children's literature with the *Underland Chronicles* fantasy series for middle-grade readers. She continued to explore themes of war and violence for a young adult audience with *The Hunger Games*. The first book in the series, published in 2008, was an instant bestseller, appealing both to teenage readers and adults. The book appeared on the *New York Times* bestseller list for over 260 consecutive weeks (more than 5 years), selling more than 100 million copies in 54 languages in 52 countries.

The New York Times Book Review thought that, "At its best the trilogy channels the political passion of *Nineteen Eighty-Four*, the memorable violence of *A Clockwork Orange*, the imaginative ambience of *The Chronicles of Narnia* and the detailed inventiveness of *Harry Potter*." In 2012, the first of four films based on the novels was released (the final book was split into two films), starring Jennifer Lawrence as Katniss. The series has earned $3 billion at the worldwide box office. Clearly, the story has resonated with audiences, particularly young people. The question is why, and whether it means anything politically.

"I really can't think about kissing when I've got a rebellion to incite"

Some commentators assumed its appeal centered on the love triangle between Katniss, Gale and fellow District 12 tribute Peeta. But this isn't the focus of the story, it's a subplot to bigger political questions, notably how to survive under an authoritarian regime, the price people are prepared to pay to bring it down and whether this corrupts the post-regime society they long for.

As Mark Fisher noted, "*The Hunger Games* is irreducibly political in a way that the *Potter* and the *Twilight* films could never be. The film's political charge depends upon the surprising intensity of its brutality. This brutality is affective rather than explicit; the amount of gore is actually quite low, and it is the prospect of pubescents murdering each other, not the sight of their doing it, which shocks. What makes *The Hunger Games* more than a workaday thriller is its disclosing of a world – a world that, as with all dystopias that connect, is a distorting mirror of our own." ("Precarious Dystopias: The Hunger Games, In Time, and Never Let Me Go", *Film Quarterly*, 2012).

Really, it's more of an anti-romance, one of the reasons the story appealed to so many young women in particular. Katniss is a rounded, believable, brave, compassionate, flawed, self-doubting character, who continues to inspire young women in particular, personally and politically, not because she's flawless, but because she isn't.

Katniss is surrounded by expectations about what she should be and how she should act. As we'll explore, the reality TV show of the Games and state spying means that Katniss and her peers are often acting for the audience, a pressure felt by young people in our own age of social media surveillance. But this means that Katniss continually distrusts the motives of Peeta in particular: does he really love her, as he declares early on in the series, or is he constructing a storyline for their survival? She even often doubts her own motivations.

"This isn't just adolescent, it's insubordination"

There's a long line of fiction popular with young people that articulates their disgust at the adult world's hypocrisies, and especially with what Holden Caulfield in *The Catcher in the Rye* famously called "phoniness." There's certainly phoniness to reject in *The Hunger Games*, and the kids do revolt against authority. But is there a real political philosophy in it?

There might be something to the idea that *The Hunger Games* appeals because it embeds familiar teenage challenges in its dystopia: disappointment with adults (from Katniss' mother's "weakness" to the authoritarian parent that is President Snow); the pressure to be likable and attractive (Katniss is told this is key to her survival in the Games); a lack of privacy; the need to make alliances, and the difficulties in deciding who can be trusted.

In how young people are contained and punished, *The Hunger Games* also reflects adult fears of adolescence as a powerful destabilizing force. Even in her hopelessness, Katniss challenges the fixed boundaries of her world, literally in the sense of temporarily escaping the Seam to hunt and feel free. But to stop here ignores the obvious themes of the story. As *Rolling Stone* put it, "It's about something pertinent, the mission to define yourself in a world that's spinning off its moral axis." It isn't a high school drama, it's a political coming-of-age story about class and conflict, for its characters, and for its audience. As Suzanne Collins has said, "I don't write about adolescence. I write about war. For adolescents."

"That's why we have to join the fight!"

Talk about great timing. The first book was published in the midst of a global financial crisis and an adult world run irresponsibly amok, from which the resulting austerity was inflicted mainly on the young, poor and minorities. Much of *The Hunger Games'* generation has lived with a lack of opportunity and growing inequalities in generational wealth and power, alongside war and terror and reality-twisting politicians. Phony isn't a strong enough word for the world they've grown up in.

The actors and director of the films were aware of the clear connections between the story and the Occupy movement, among other protests, that were taking place while they were filming the first movie. Donald Sutherland, who plays President Snow, wrote an extended letter to director Gary Ross about power and how it applied to his role, including asserting that the trilogy is an allegory of "this imperial power, this oligarchy of the multi-rich, the 0.1%."

As many reviewers have noted, Collins is a very deliberate world builder, with lots of historical references and allusions. But the story really resonates because it looks forward. The future in the story isn't really so futuristic, it's fast oncoming social fact. Young people are offered up as sacrifices for the elite-controlled state. They face a punitive and divisive economic system, environmental collapse, authoritarian populist politics, sophisticated media manipulation and total surveillance. For Americans and others who don't recognize the dystopia that's already here, let alone the one to come, it's either because they feel safely ensconced in the Capitol or because they've already accepted its Hobbesian propaganda.

Perhaps one day they too will win the economic lottery and be bathed in riches, at least they hope. In the story, however, as an audience we're positioned not with the Capitol or its most favored districts, but in the degrading hopelessness of District 12. We're with the kids.

"I'm going to be the Mockingjay"

The Capitol's ritual televised sacrifice of tributes, the watching of which is mandatory, demonstrates its domination of the districts. The Games promote a brutal competitive individualism that seeks to obliterate all other values, and humanity itself. They exert the Capitol's control beyond its economic exploitation of the districts, into peoples' ability to envision an alternative future free of domination. However, the spectacle of the Games also creates an opportunity for the subversion of the Capitol's story of subjection for the "good of the nation," ultimately into one of personal sacrifice, of love, demonstrating a different kind of unity. This is the spark that Katniss sets off when she volunteers.

The power of stories and symbols runs through *The Hunger Games*. The Mockingjay, an unintended cross-breed of a bird genetically-engineered by the Capitol, becomes a symbol of defiance personified in Katniss herself. Later, using Katniss, the rebels mount their own propaganda war. The struggle that takes up most of the original series is not the physical war to overthrow the Capitol, it's the propaganda war of stories and symbols between the rebels and the rulers. Force is never enough to quell a population. But propaganda can be subverted against power.

"They just want a good show, that's all they want"

We might be suspicious of Hollywood selling us rebeltainment, even clever meta-stories that critique how rebels use storytelling to sell their revolution. There must be a catch. Does the story depict capitalism correctly? Is the revolution depoliticized? Is it counter-revolutionary? In the circular logic prevalent in critical cultural commentary, it must be, because it's corporations selling it to us. The criticism is that *The Hunger Games* and its imitators might represent some of the fears, frustrations and anxieties of today's precarious young proletarians, but it doesn't really name the system of oppression or its possible replacement.

Even if this were true, if Hollywood is the creative Capitol, we can claim and subvert its stories. Katniss introduces a new story to the Games, of defiance in place of deference, cooperation instead of competitive individualism, self-sacrifice rather than subservience. Once these seeds have been sown, it's the Capitol that becomes terrified of their reaping. It scrambles to regain the initiative by attempting to assimilate Katniss and Peeta's alliance (with, yes, some reality TV game playing on their part as well) into a sentimental story of "star-crossed lovers." Neatly anticipating some of the misguided commentary on *The Hunger Games* as just a teen love triangle, the Capitol desperately tries to depoliticize them.

It's better surely to act like the rebels in the story and recognize when some useful revolutionary symbolism has been thrown our way. Or as Mark Fisher ("Precarious Dystopias") puts it, "[I]f blockbusters about class revolution perform their ultimate ideological function – maintaining business as usual – by encouraging our cynical distance from those underlying fantasies, the truly subversive thing is not to disregard the dream but to stick to the desire that sustains it."

"You provided a spark that, left unattended, may grow to an inferno that destroys Panem"

Just like protesters around the world have done. We've already mentioned Hong Kong. In 2014, young protesters against the military junta's coup in Thailand also used the three-fingered salute as a symbol of solidarity and defiance. Like the Capitol, the Thai authorities recognized the power of popular symbols and banned it (some protesters were detained for defying the ban). It didn't stop protesters using it again in rallies in Bangkok in December 2019.

Campaigners too have drawn on *The Hunger Games*. The Harry Potter Alliance, which uses popular fiction to engage fans in activism, has created successive campaigns using the series. These started in 2012 with Hunger Is Not A Game (focusing on food poverty) and returned with the release of *Catching Fire* (the second book and film) as Odds In Our Favor. The latter tackled economic inequality and the culture of silence around poverty. The Alliance's We Are The Districts initiative flooded social media with statistics about hunger and other forms of structural violence, from workplace injuries and deaths, and a lack of mental health services, to punitive "welfare to work" programs and revenge incarceration.

Many other local groups have drawn on the series to challenge poverty, criminal justice policy, police racism and brutality, homelessness and environmental destruction. International development NGOs have often used the series to frame issues of poverty, hunger, youth unemployment, unfair and exploitative trade practices, and growing global inequality.

Just as Katniss despairs at the start of the story, the Capitol depends on us believing that change is impossible, that the system is too strong. But unbeknown to her and Gale and Peeta, the revolution is about to begin, the districts are more ready to revolt than they know, and the Capitol is more vulnerable than they assume. Sometimes it just needs someone to supply the spark.

"If desperate times call for desperate measures, then I am free to act as desperately as I wish"

Which is why *The Hunger Games* is about containment, and the fundamental fear that Capitol elites have about the people of the districts. Katniss, the other tributes, the districts, even the victors – all are constantly contained and herded, by fences, borders, Peacekeepers, artificial arenas and deadly hazards, pervasive propaganda and reality TV productions.

Today's young people will live in a future of walls, of containment driven by collapse, environmental destruction, scarcity and a sociopathic elder elite's fear of losing power. More than 3 decades after the fall of the Berlin Wall, young people are unconstrained by fears of authoritarian "socialism." New walls need to be constructed, of individualism, intolerance, hopelessness and passivity. Working out what's real and what's Capitol propaganda will be crucial, the first step to surviving the coming hunger games. And let's remember that the Capitol wouldn't bother with its propaganda if it didn't fundamentally fear us.

In *The Hunger Games*, Katniss is the last person to recognize her significance, and our potential to bring down the walls. The Capitol and the rebels identify her power long before she does. What she wakes up to is not the full horror of the system, she's more than aware of that. No, what she comes to understand is that, in the world of Panem, survival is unavoidably a revolutionary act.

Part I

The Districts

Chapter 1

"District 12, where you can starve to death in safety"

"There were no real lives, because we never had any real choice"

Katniss lives where the downtrodden try to survive in a country controlled by others. We experience her alienation, self-doubt and anger. The skills she's developed for survival will help her during the Games, but she has no hope of escaping her world, let alone changing it. In an early conversation with Gale, he says they could run away, live in the woods. Given their hunting skills, they could make it. Katniss doesn't know how to respond ("The idea is so preposterous").

As Mark Fisher ("Precarious Dystopias") notes: "Up until [the] climactic moment, *The Hunger Games* is striking for the fatalism of its lead characters, something that is all the more remarkable given the personal courage and self-sacrifice that they show. They think like slaves, taking it for granted that the Capitol's power cannot be broken."

But this isn't the whole story. Like the forgotten districts of our world, there's a strength, defiance and hidden radicalness here as well, if only we'd recognize it.

"The question is, what are you going to do?"

To Ernst Bloch in *The Principle of Hope*, if hunger "increases uninterrupted, satisfied by no certain bread, then it suddenly changes. The body-ego then becomes rebellious...It seeks to change the situation which has caused its empty stomach, its hanging head...[H]unger transforms itself, having been taught, into an explosive force against the prison of deprivation."

The Hunger Games is the story about how a revolution

happens. In our world the conditions are seemingly present for revolution: massive and increasing inequality; ostentatious displays of wealth by elites; the widespread belief that ruling classes serve only themselves; little expectation of meaningful action to address poverty and inequality; and elite's reliance on propaganda and policing that are increasingly disdained by the populace.

But neither in the story nor our world do we anticipate that revolution is coming. The common leftist explanation is that poverty and ignorance, especially a lack of class consciousness, are obstacles to revolt. If only people recognized their own strength, they'd sweep away the system, but it's the system that keeps them poor and ignorant. And yet, our journey into District 12 suggests that things are a bit more complicated than this.

"We're strong too. Just in a different way"

District 12 is the smallest and poorest district. Even among the other districts, it's a laughing stock. Katniss suggests it's largely ignored because of its apparent lack of revolutionary fervor, although it's still exploited by the Capitol to the point of starvation. But while there's little belief in revolutionary possibility here, there is in survival. There's a pride in resilience, and a desire for dignity.

As in our world, this doesn't automatically translate into rebellion. More often, inequality induces exhaustion and resignation. Yet later, as dissent spreads, the Capitol will come to recognize the strength of the districts' defiance, embodied most of all in Katniss herself.

"There are lots of underdogs. And I think if you could see them, you would not root for them either"

But to begin with, there's a fundamental condescension about District 12. No one expects the rebellion to start here, in this backward, beaten down little district. And no wonder. As

President Snow's conversation with the Head Gamemaker Seneca captures (shown only in the film adaptation), elites despise those below them. The elite's classism – contempt for poor and working-class people – justifies why they can be sacrificed in the Games, just as they are in the mines, the factories and the fields. (However, we learn in the prequel *The Ballad of Songbirds and Snakes* that Snow knows District 12 more than most: when he was younger, he was assigned as a mentor to the tribute from the district.)

Classism is the last acceptable form of discrimination. It normalizes poverty, because the "underdogs" ("underclass") are assumed to be lazy, indolent and irresponsible. In fact, their poverty is created by the Capitol, by its heavily policed economic system and class division, then they're blamed for their "dysfunction" when it's the system that's responsible.

"The lives of district people – they mean less than nothing to them"

Katniss describes how starvation is normal in her district, but it's never an official cause of death. We look away too, but in the richest country on earth, hunger is real. Nearly 49 million Americans, including more than 16 million children, live in households that lack food. More children are hungry than adults: 1 in 5 go hungry at some point during any year. A total of 45 million Americans rely on food stamps. Two-thirds of these benefits go to households with children, and 45 percent of recipients are children. But around 1 in 5 families with children experiencing food insecurity don't even qualify for assistance-based programs.

In the United States, hunger was virtually eliminated in the 1970s. Now, after 40 years of a right-wing economic regime, it's back. The number of people going hungry has grown dramatically. The present levels represent a fivefold rise since the late 1960s, with an increase of 57 percent since the late 1990s alone.

Hunger is particularly prevalent in the districts. A total of 15 percent of families living in rural areas experience food insecurity, compared with nearly 12 percent living in suburban and metropolitan areas. People of color are also disproportionately affected. Black and Latino children experience hunger at double the rate of white children. More than one in four black households and one in five Latino households lack food security, compared to one in ten white households.

It's not just absolute hunger, it's also access to good food. A "food desert" is an area that lacks suppliers of fresh poultry, fish and meat, fruit and vegetables. A total of 23.5 million people live in one, which is probably an underestimate. Nearly half of them are low-income households, while a fifth of rural areas are food deserts.

Conservatives attack such statistics, claiming that this can't possibly be true in such a rich country. It probably feels that way from the full tables of the Capitol.

"We both know I'm not above killing children"

Hunger is also increasing globally. Worldwide, 821 million people go hungry, one in every nine people on the planet. Over 150 million children are stunted by hunger. Close to 2 billion people suffer from micronutrient malnutrition, a "hidden hunger" because it's less visible but which causes many of the same health problems. This is particularly detrimental to young children, women of childbearing age and the poorest populations in developing countries. It costs millions of lives each year and prevents an even greater number from escaping poverty.

Conflict and climate change have caused much of this deterioration (discussed more in Chapter 3). Other factors include unfair trade practices which cost developing countries at least $300 billion a year (far more than they receive in aid), and increase food and energy prices, gender inequality and land acquisition by corporations and governments which displaces the poor. It's not a question of inevitable scarcity, we produce enough food to feed everyone. The problem is wealth and power which hoards resources for itself.

"It was all for the Games"

Katniss was being ironic, as she often is. In District 12, you can't even starve to death in safety.

It might seem horribly honest for a regime to call its primary propaganda tool the Hunger Games. But it's entirely deliberate. As Suzanne Collins has said, "The socio-political overtones of *The Hunger Games* were very intentionally created to characterize current and past world events, including the use of hunger as a weapon to control populations" ("Interview by James Blasingame", *Journal of Adolescent & Adult Literacy*, May 2009).

The Games are a reminder, a threat and a demonstration of domination. Naming them is about power. It's not meant to generate support for the system, but to crush any humane alternative. As Katniss recognizes, it's the Capitol's way of saying, "Look how we take your children and sacrifice them and there's nothing you can do." You can't even protest, let alone rebel.

How the Capitol justifies its regime is really not so different from how some people promote capitalism here: how it disciplines us to work or starve, punishes the "indolent," and rewards the "winners." If we think the Capitol is too honest, we forget how in our world apologists for capitalism also celebrate its cruel and controlling methods.

"Whatever it takes to break you"

Collins indicts a country in which an elite suffer sickness through overeating while most ache with hunger. The rulers starve the districts, and it works. Hunger forces people to focus on survival. Katniss knows what they're taught in school about Panem isn't the whole story, but she can't afford to care ("Whatever the truth is, I don't see how it will help me get food on the table"). By keeping people hungry, elites ensure that they don't have the time or energy to rebel (as noted, hunting in the districts is outlawed).

Immiseration and unemployment are a deliberate political strategy of capitalism. Scarcity induces fear, of not being able to survive, but also of each other. In survival, we put ourselves and our families over the possibility of solidarity and social change.

"If I'm going to die, I want to still be me"

As James Baldwin wrote: "Anyone who has ever struggled with poverty knows how extremely expensive it is to be poor" ("Fifth Avenue, Uptown: A Letter from Harlem", *Esquire*, July 1960).

In the world of *The Hunger Games*, tesserae is a system of food rationing offered by the Capitol. Families with a child aged 12-18 can sign up. A single tessera is worth one year's (meager) supply of grain and oil for a single person. Even so, they come at a cost: the child's name is added to the reaping lottery an additional time for every tessera claimed that year. These entries are cumulative; if tesserae are claimed year after year, the chances of being reaped increase dramatically. In Panem, poverty directly increases the chances of dying.

Tesserae are also a mark of class. They're predominantly claimed in the poorest districts, indeed District 12 is considered the poorest because it has the highest proportion of people taking tesserae. This marker also operates within the districts. From a family without a father, living in the poorest part of the poorest district, Katniss has taken tesserae every year since she turned 12. Peeta, selected for the Games alongside Katniss, whose family owns a bakery, has never needed to.

This echoes our own punitive welfare systems. Not only are such benefits often insufficient to live on, they also come at a cost, to punish the poor with time-wasting, bureaucratic requirements to find low paid, insecure work. Such policing of the poor also distracts from the fact that the majority of welfare recipients are in work but on poverty wages. In the US, most households receiving government assistance are headed by a working adult. In some industries, about half the workforce relies on welfare.

Historically, such punitive "welfare" rests on an engineered division which dates back centuries between the deserving "respectable working class" and the undeserving "underclass." The former work hard, keep their homes and families clean, attend church, maintain sobriety, and otherwise adhere to middle-class morals (it doesn't stop them being poor though). The undeserving poor supposedly "earn" their poverty by not working hard enough, but also by rejecting middle-class "morality." We'll ignore for the moment that the most feckless residents of Panem reside in its Capitol.

"Never let them see you bleed"

Poverty and precarity also have a psychological effect. As Eldar Shafir and Sendhil Mullainathan explain in their book *Scarcity: Why Having Too Little Means So Much,* a lack of resources forces our brains to focus on alleviating pressing shortages and reduces the mental bandwidth available to address other needs, plan ahead and solve problems.

Hunger has a particular impact on children. Food insecurity contributes to toxic stress. This can affect brain development, information processing, and learning. Severe hunger is associated with anxiety and depression in children, and depressive disorders and suicidality in adolescents. Lack of food also causes poor health, including stomach aches, headaches and colds. Physically, severe hunger predicts chronic illness among both preschool and school-age children. Psychologically, hungry children often feel shame. So many children are playing the hunger games everyday.

"I just can't afford to think like that"

It's not just hunger. Economic conditions trap many people into insecurity, precarity, jobs they hate, lives of survival rather than possibility.

Take debt, a key means of containing people. Young Americans owe more than $1 trillion in debt, mostly student loans, but also auto loans, credit cards, mortgages and other forms of consumer credit. Millennials on average carry $27,800 in personal debt (for older millennials it's $42,000), and Generation Z on average $14,000. Partly as a result of declining opportunity and poor jobs, one-third of borrowers who graduated between 2006 and 2011 have defaulted.

Only 28 percent of Americans are considered "financially healthy." A total of 17 percent are "financially vulnerable," meaning they struggle with nearly all financial aspects of their lives, and 55 percent are just "financially coping," struggling with some but not all of their financial lives. A total of 44 percent say their expenses have exceeded their income in the past year and use credit to make ends meet. A total of 42 percent have no retirement savings.

Again, debt is political. As described in David Graeber's *Debt: The First 5,000 Years*, the struggle between rich and poor has largely taken the form of conflicts between creditors and debtors, from slavery and land seizures, to modern forms of debt. Economic life originally depended on "social currencies" based on routine non-market interactions within a community. This created an "everyday communism" based on mutual expectation, equality and reciprocity (we'll come back to this in Chapter 9). This imprecise, informal, community-building debt of "human economies" was replaced by precise debts enforced through compulsion and sometimes violence.

Debt also enslaves countries. It causes poverty, malnutrition, loots public resources, slashes the money available for education and health services, and leads to social instability and violence.

As ever, it's the poorest and most vulnerable, especially children, who are hurt most.

In Panem, the Hunger Games are the annual reminder of the debt "owed" by the districts for the first rebellion. But like our debts, what's owed is increasingly unpayable, and anyway, the Capitol's elites don't really want these debts to be settled. They like keeping control.

"We have all one enemy, and it's the Capitol!"

Panem isn't a democracy. But given its terrible conditions, why haven't the districts rebelled against the Capitol? Or in our world, since some of us live in democracies, why do some working-class people vote against their own interests, or not vote at all (nevermind not revolt against the system) – the so-called "Great Paradox"?

Often, this is explained by "false consciousness." But this isn't an issue in District 12 (it may be in some of the more favored districts closer to the Capitol). The residents of the district know that the system is grossly unfair, but hunger strips people of energy, dignity, comradeship and any sense of the future. Indeed, in *The Hunger Games*, it's an act of kindness involving bread that is the seed that later sparks the revolution. It's being fed, not hunger, that eventually leads to change.

"I guess there are no rules about what a person can do to another person"

Inequality has been rising for years since the establishment of the hunger games of neoliberalism (deregulation, privatization and "trickle down economics") from the 1980s onwards. And yet before the global financial crisis of 2007-8, the neoliberal argument was heralded as unquestionable, as secure as the Capitol's grip on Panem.

The Hunger Games, the first book, was released on September 14, 2008, the same day investment bank Lehman Brothers declared bankruptcy and the crisis entered its most acute phase. This was an accident of timing but also, for a series that depicts a world of gross inequality and elite corruption, prescient. The crisis was in many ways the outcome of inequality; the only way ordinary people could afford a home was courtesy of fundamentally fake financial instruments, based on income they didn't have and interest rates they couldn't afford.

But even this crisis didn't spark revolt. Supported by its propagandists, the Capitol was said to have "won" the story regarding the causes of the crisis and its required consequences: that the rich need to be protected while the poor are punished. It was class war, by the rich, on the poor, as blatant as the cruel regime of the Capitol.

Why was austerity accepted? It wasn't really. Just as the Capitol tries to convince the districts that everyone accepts, even celebrates, the Hunger Games, so our elites try to convince us that we all agree with the necessity of punishing the poor. And scarcity also erodes solidarity. Our Capitols blame minorities, the poor, the vulnerable, immigrants. It's an effective strategy, so much so that it can make people seemingly support the policies that harm them, as Jonathan Metzl demonstrates in *Dying of Whiteness: How the Politics of Racial Resentment Is Killing America's Heartland*.

As Katniss notes, "After the reaping, everyone is supposed to celebrate. And many do, out of relief that their children have been spared for another year. But at least two families will pull their shutters, lock their doors, and try to figure out how they will survive the painful weeks to come." But the rest of us think, thank god we've survived, for now. Thank god we're not *them*.

"Everyone knows I have a scar here"

District 12 is in Appalachia, one of the most deprived regions in the US, and one of the most maligned. Suzanne Collins chose it for a reason: it's looked down on as irredeemedly poor and backward, ignorant and violent. *The Hunger Games* illustrates how we shame the poor.

Home to 25 million people, Appalachia runs from the southern tip of New York to northern Alabama and Georgia. Culturally, however, it refers to the central and southern part of the Appalachian mountain range, from the Blue Ridge mountains, southwest to the Great Smoky mountains. Since its recognition as a distinctive region in the late nineteenth century, Appalachia has been subject to enduring distortions regarding the temperament and behavior of its people.

Katniss is one of its downtrodden "white trash," seemingly apolitical, resigned, insular, ignorant. They're not even working class, they're detached, a subspecies. This condescension is reflected in some leftist misreadings of *The Hunger Games*. Katniss can't be a hero because she's insufficiently political, so the series too must be hollow Hollywood nonsense. But this is to neglect her true politics and agency, just like the Capitol, and Panem's revolutionary leaders, later do as well.

"Shame isn't a strong enough word for what I feel"

This shame becomes internalized. Richard Sennett and Jonathan Cobb described the "hidden injuries of class" in their 1972 book – the multiple ways in which working-class people are taught their lives are less valuable. Richer people, we're told, have better characters and are more rational. Later, in the Capitol, Katniss is told how to comport herself if she wants to be accepted. But as Sennett and Cobb argue, whatever our manners, a humane society can't be built on the inhumanities of class.

Katniss is constantly self-doubting and thinks she's fundamentally bad in some way, selfish, an imposter. At the root of this, as Alice Miller suggests, neglected and punished children rationalize their suffering by reasoning that they deserve it, that they're worthy of hatred. As Miller states, the child consequently "belittles her feelings to protect herself."

Even when Katniss does "rise up" in society, in effect and for a short time, by surviving the Hunger Games, she feels the same, worse even, about being unworthy. Moreover, as she notes, the ultimate humiliation is that the Capitol forces the districts to treat the Games as a festivity celebrating their own servitude. The Games are an instrument of class power, and class humiliation.

"Trapped for days, years, centuries maybe. Dead, but not allowed to die"

There's no reason why Appalachia should be poor, endowed as it is with abundant natural resources. The cause of its destitution is that, like the districts, it's been ruthlesly exploited by outsiders. As Tim Wise (*Under the Affluence: Shaming the Poor, Praising the Rich and Sacrificing the Future of America*) suggests, far from a culture of poverty, it's a culture of predatory affluence that's to blame.

What the Capitol's apologists erase from the Appalachian landscape are the business actors who seized its timber and minerals, fought its coal-mining unions and corraled its people. Echoing the Capitol's control of Panem, this started generations ago. As recorded in Wilma Dunaway's *The First American Frontier*, British crown and colonial authorities granted huge tracts of land to court favorites, Virginia planters and Eastern capitalists. By the beginning of the nineteenth century, absentee investors owned more than 90 percent of West Virginia and three-quarters of eastern Kentucky. Central Appalachia's extractive industries allowed the region's natural wealth to be redistributed to shareholders in faraway metropolises (only in the 1970s did states pass laws that claimed a share of the earnings from coal extraction).

As Nancy Isenberg recounts in *White Trash: The 400-Year Untold History of Class in America*, England used the American colonies as dumping grounds for those thought of as indolent. Outposts such as Jamestown, the first permanent English settlement in the Americas and the colonial capital from 1616 until 1699, exploited unfree laborers (servants, slaves and children), who were regarded as human waste.

Puritanism also helped to reinforce rigid class divisions. The core of the church represented an Elect, much like the pamprered, privileged residents of the Capitol. This was regarded as a natural condition: inevitable, god-given, even scientific. The migrants in the districts were met with harsh labor conditions, and frequently death. Starvation was common. Debt among indentured servants and slaves (often a "payment" for Atlantic passage) was passed onto spouses and children if parents died, which they often did through overwork. If children did survive, they could be dragooned into being soldiers and sailors for the colonial reserve army and sent to die in England's wars.

No wonder many migrant peasant farmers fled into the mountains and the forests, beyond the reach of the law. Without legal protection, they could only depend on themselves to survive.

As Isenberg notes, historical myths are made possible only by forgetting. Like the "national unity" the Capitol promotes through its Hunger Games, the idea of America as a "shining city on a hill" was only created later to reinforce elite power. After 400 years, descendents might regard their tough existence as normal, and are understandably hostile to government. Such dispossession teaches its victims to accept not only that life is hard, but also contradictory, meaningless and lacking in hope.

"Divided, they stay fallen"

A critical way of disempowering working-class communities has been to destroy, sometimes using violence, their forms of solidarity, most obviously through trade unions. This has particularly hurt areas like Appalachia, leaving them prey to exploitation and extraction, which is of course the aim.

Just as Katniss knows little about Panem's first rebellion,

we're lied to about our own histories. How many of us know for example that "redneck," now a smear for working-class rural reactionary whites, used to denote a radical working-class organization, based on the coal-mining union members who wore red bandanas for solidarity? Or about the Battle of Blair Mountain in 1921, the largest labor uprising in US history and one of the largest armed uprisings since the Civil War?

This battle occurred in Logan County, West Virginia, as part of the Coal Wars, a series of early twentieth century labor disputes in Appalachia. Coal miners marched south from the state capitol at Charleston, West Virginia, toward the anti-union counties of Logan, Mingo and McDowell. Their aim was to end the notorious Mine Guard System, which enabled the coal companies, backed by private forces of armed guards, to rule the coalfields as a police state.

Most West Virginia miners lived in poverty in disease-ridden "company towns" (camps) without elected officials or independent police forces. Mine guards manned machine gun turrets to quell any attempts at rebellion. Miners and their families rented cramped company houses, were paid in company currency, and bought goods at company stores. Company representatives even controlled the mail, removing any "subversive" pro-union literature.

The miners confronted 3000 lawmen and strikebreakers in a 5-day gun battle in which 1 million rounds were fired, more than a hundred people were killed and many more were arrested. The miners wore their red bandanas to identify themselves against the white-armband-wearing, industry-funded opposition. The battle ended after the US Army arrived by presidential order and dispersed the miners, dealing a decade-long setback to the movement.

"There's plenty of blame to go around"

As in Panem, the defeat of the rebellion and its deliberate

forgetting has led to decades of exploitation and punishment for working people. The war has continued ever since. Over the past 40 years, neoliberal economics which serves the interests of elites has further weakened the power of workers, including through a model of globalization that promotes outsourcing, promoted by trade agreements like NAFTA that undercut domestic jobs.

Deindustrialization has been traumatic for these communities, a collective and individual suffering. More than 1300 non-metro counties in the US have lost population since 2010, partly as a result of job growth that is less than one-third that of urban areas. Since 2001, the number of manufacturing jobs in rural areas has declined by more than 20 percent. Every year, more of the remaining jobs are concentrated in poorly paid service sectors. And with fewer small businesses, people are increasingly reliant for work from big corporations. But the Walmarts and Amazons are really just the latest colonists of these districts, huge machines designed to extract money back to their faraway Capitols.

"Destroying things is much easier than making them"

In *The Hunger Games* we see Katniss' love for the outdoors, in contrast to the environmental destruction of the districts and the waste created by the consumerist Capitol. As with people, the environment is just something to be exploited. The Capitol has no love of nature; it even creates its own in its Games arenas, artifical environments full of hazards and mutts (genetically-engineered monsters).

Our Capitol treats its districts in the same way. For generations, severe poverty and hardship, along with psychological damage, has caused huge health problems in Appalachia. Now, so called "diseases of despair," including opioid addiction, are prevalent. By 2015, West Virginia's rate of opioid related overdose death for those aged 15-64 was more than three times higher than the rest of the country, while Appalachian Kentucky's was more than twice the rate. McDowell County, in West Virginia's southern coalfields, has the highest opioid overdose rate in America. Residents of central Appalachia report feeling mentally unhealthy 25 percent more than the average American. Nearly a fifth of the area's Medicare beneficiaries suffer from depression.

There's another reason for such poor physical and mental health. The historic dispossession of land by the Capitol means that distant owners have been happy to destroy the environment, while residents have lacked the legal and political power to resist. Working-class communities and people of color are often in the frontline of pollution. Due to entrenched segregation, zoning that privileges wealthier communities, and the power of corporations against local representatives, as Dorceta Taylor notes in *Toxic Communities* there are neighborhoods so polluted that just living in them is hazardous.

In Appalachia, mountaintops are blasted off in search of coal, and lax regulations allow companies to leak toxic chemicals into the water with impunity. Since the 1990s, half of the region's coal has come from mountaintop removal, which has destroyed more than 500 mountains. The pollutants used also kill rivers and streams. In 2012, the Environmental Protection Agency estimated that 1.4 million acres of native forest had been destroyed, which is highly unlikely to recover on the broken soils left behind. It's like bombing a district.

As with economic exploitation, this destruction relies on shaming. As Naomi Klein notes, lightly regulated industrial capitalism and the fossil fuels it relies on are so inherently dirty that they require people and places that can be sacrificed to dump the waste. As recently as the 1970s, scientists advising the US government openly referred to certain parts of the country as designated "national sacrifice areas." As Klein suggests, "There must be theories of othering to justify sacrificing an entire geography – theories about the people who lived there being so poor and backward that their lives and culture don't deserve protection…[Y]ou can't have a system built on sacrificial places and sacrificial people unless intellectual theories that justify their sacrifice exist and persist." ("Let Them Drown, The Violence of Othering in a Warming World", *London Review of Books*, June 2016.)

"Just because you come from District 12 is no excuse to ignore you"

Given all of this history of disempowerment, it's not surprising that West Virginia frequently has the lowest voter turnout in the US. And yet the central Appalachian coalfields were one of Donald Trump's biggest strongholds of support in the 2016 presidential election.

Divide and rule explains part of this. Of course poor people are susceptible to being told that another group is "below" them. But the notion of working-class people as mere dupes for demagogues is another shaming of the districts, blaming them for their own punishment. Most working-class voters didn't support Trump. In fact, the white working class is under-represented among Trump voters; his supporters are disproportionally college-educated whites. Moreover, the media's frequent depiction of the working class as white, male and right-wing ignores the much greater diversity of the actual working class, who remain largely invisible.

As Nadine Hubbs points out in *Rednecks, Queers, & Country Music*, there's a long history of elites blaming racial violence on poor whites. But the institutional racism of banks denying mortgages to people of color, employers not hiring them and landlords exploiting them is generally not carried out by poor and working-class whites but by white middle-class professionals – not by the districts but by the Capitol.

"For there to be betrayal, there would have to have been trust first"

Other working-class people disengage because they didn't

see the possibility of real change. Much more than bastions of Trump-loving conservatism, rural communities are home to people who feel a contempt for the status quo that persists whichever party is in power.

Given the exploitation they experience, the residents of the districts are understandably suspicious of the Capitol's political games. Decades of decline have continued unabated. They know that elite liberals benefit from the system; why trust their promises to "reform" what serves them well? As Thomas Frank has long argued (in *What's the Matter With Kansas?*, among other books), the Democrats are a class party, but the class is increasingly a satisfied, prosperous professional class who aren't all that concerned about growing inequality. When commentators wonder why some people vote against their own interests, they're asking the wrong question.

Most of all, if your experience of the state is typically one of coercion and humiliation, why would you trust liberals when they claim that the Capitol, run by many of the same people, is here to help? The revolution that working-class people want is not to replace one set of leaders with another, it's to remove the shaming from the state and the control of corporations from their lives. But no one's offering them that, not yet.

"Excellent! You almost look like a human being now!"

In contrast to the Capitol's propaganda, in *The Hunger Games* we're presented with different personification of the underclass. Katniss is decent, strong, brave and kind. She's an honest working-class woman who suffers incredible hardship but endures. She might seem passive and resigned, but she's also decisive and acts swiftly.

And she's not alone. At the start of *The Hunger Games*, when Prim "wins" the lottery and Katniss volunteers, the anger in District 12 is evident. When the crowd are asked to clap, they salute Katniss with three fingers held up. It's both a sign of resistance against the Capitol, and of solidarity with her. What will become a gesture of rebellion starts in compassion. It isn't explicitly revolutionary, but it is unavoidably political. It's a sign of working-class unity with real meaning in her community, a symbol of district pride assumed long since lost. That's why the later revolutionary leadership will use Katniss as a figurehead (while at the same time denying her any real power, but we'll get to that).

President Snow may regard them as underdogs. But this means that the people of the districts are underestimated. It will turn out to be a terrible mistake for the Capitol to make.

Chapter 2

"They messed us up pretty good, didn't they?"

"Welcome, welcome. The time has come to select one courageous young man and woman..."

If class and poverty are the first major themes of *The Hunger Games*, the second is trauma and coping, especially as experienced by young people. As well as enforced poverty, we're presented with the corrosive effects of cruelty, terror and fear, powerlessness and passivity.

Most obviously, we see how children from poor communities are forced to fight to the death in a gruesome reality TV show for the entertainment of the rich. On top of systemic poverty and inequality, this is intended to numb a pauperized populace. It seems to work.

The generation coming into adulthood now are often referred to as Gen Z (Generation Z). They're typically understood to have been born between 1997 and 2012. The oldest of them might vaguely remember the end of the twentieth century. Some of them will live to see the twenty-second century. *The Hunger Games* is their story; they're the tributes of our world.

According to some calculations, Gen Z has surpassed millennials (Gen Y), Gen X and baby boomers as the largest age group globally. But as we'll see, they've been increasingly subject to containment, literally in some cases, and also through mockery and mischaracterizations. The oldest of them, perhaps their older sisters and brothers first, will have read Suzanne Collins' series and then watched the films at the same time they were coming to their own comprehension of the state of the world. A society controlled by a corrupt elder elite, albeit heightened and dramatized; the story felt, still feels, like it captures an essential truth. As does its depiction of what a world like this does to the young people who live in it.

In creating her fictional world, Collins reflects many of the prevailing anxieties of young people today. No wonder *The Hunger Games* speaks so strongly to them. It suggests, much more than most generational commentary and analysis, what's really traumatizing the kids.

"Well, there is this one girl..."

Katniss epitomizes this trauma. Even before the Games, she's desensitized. She describes the suffering of the districts, but there are no feelings attached. She's continually repressing her emotions, shielding her vulnerability, wary of connections and anything that isn't self-sufficiency. Katniss is always ready to help others, but doesn't want to rely on anyone else. How could she, in her world?

Katniss' father is dead, her mother is dead-to-the-world, suffering from debilitating depression. It's down to Katniss to take care of herself, her little sister and her mother. She seems to cope with poverty and deprivation pretty well, but it's a life not being lived. She can't even feel joy in music: "In our world, I rank music somewhere between hair ribbons and rainbows in terms of usefulness. At least a rainbow gives you a tip about the weather."

Katniss is alienated from herself, to the extent she's internalized the Capitol's hateful propaganda. She thinks she's a fundamentally horrible person, unworthy of love. She doesn't believe anyone else could love her either. Much later in the story, a brainwashed Peeta "proves" this to her, that stripped of his love, she's an emotionless rat who cares only for her own survival ("Finally, he can see me for who I really am").

What lies underneath this is deep grief. The cruelest crime committed by the Capitol is not the way it kidnaps children to participate in the Games, terrible as that is. It's the way the entire system steals from children any sense of psychological safety. As Alice Miller stated (*The Drama of the Gifted Child*): "In what is described as depression and experienced as emptiness, futility, fear of impoverishment, and loneliness can usually be recognized as the tragic loss of the self in childhood, manifested as the total alienation from the self in the adult."

Of course, *The Hunger Games* is an extreme story. But in these respects it reflects the feelings of young people today, one of the reasons for its resonance with them. And yet, Katniss will come to recognize she's not to blame, that it's the system, and that recovery and healing, personal and collective, will only be possible if the true source of terror is confronted.

"I'm not very good at making friends"

Anxiety, depression and suicide among young people are soaring. According to the US National Institute of Mental Health, young adults aged 18-25 years have the highest prevalence (25.8 percent) of any mental illness compared to older age groups. The same pattern goes for serious mental illness, meaning a mental disorder which substantially interferes with or limits one or more major life activities. A total of 7.5 percent of young adults experience these conditions, compared to only 2.7 percent for those aged 50 and older.

This has continued to worsen since the global financial crisis. Drawing on the National Survey on Drug Use and Health, more people in their 20s exhibit signs of major depressive disorder, such as feelings of fatigue, worthlessness and guilt, than the same age group did just a decade ago. Those reporting experiencing a major depressive episode in the last year have increased 52 percent between 2005-2017 among adolescents aged 12-17, and 63 percent among young adults aged 18-25 between 2009-2017. Serious psychological distress in the last month and suicide-related outcomes (suicidal ideation, attempts and deaths by suicide) in the last year have also increased among young people aged 18-25 between 2008-2017, including a 71 percent increase in the former.

The chances of a person in this age group dying by suicide is now greater than by homicide. Among younger adults aged 25-44, death rates rose 21 percent for whites and blacks and 13 percent for hispanics between 2012-2017, according to the Centers for Disease Control. Most young victims in this age group died of injuries, including from drug overdoses and suicides.

And perhaps surprisingly for a generation often characterized as hyper-connected, multiple surveys suggest that loneliness is pervasive among millennials and Gen Z.

"I realize, for the first time, how very lonely I've been in the arena"

Older commentators have found some strange ways to explain this crisis. Young people are spoiled, sensitive snowflakes who lack resilience. A trophy generation, too praised, entitled, narcissistic. No wonder they suffer from Peter Pan syndrome, not wanting to grow up. They've been coddled in a childish utopia.

The truth is the opposite. To start with, Alice Miller would immediately recognize how this represents victim blaming. Children and young people who are abused are often told they're too sensitive when they express their pain, that they need to "toughen up," even that their abusers are "doing them a favor" by preparing them for a brutal world (it's that Hobbesianism again). As Alfie Kohn (*The Myth of the Spoiled Child*) notes, even many liberals seem to agree with the conservative critique that adults are both under- and over-parenting at the same time – too permissive, but somehow also too interfering.

If there is over-parenting, much of it might come from parents feeling the need to prepare their children for a world in which competition is ever-increasing and near-perfection is required – in school tests, university entrance exams, even in sports and "recreational" activities.

Further, Malcolm Harris (*Kids These Days*) suggests that what he calls the "Student Debt Industrial Complex" represents a huge subconscious shift to regarding human beings as capital. The marketization of education has fostered the construction of "neoliberal subjects," individuals who are increasingly transferring economic risks onto themselves. Young people's lives are viewed as investments in "human capital" that will yield returns years later. Of course, the market hasn't held up its end of the bargain, but anyway, they've come to be seen, and sometimes see themselves, as products, the ultimate alienation.

While young people of every generation face challenges, today's have been taught that resources, whether economic, educational or environmental, are limited and that they'll have to fight for them, a mental hunger games they have internalized to the point of sickness. In the parenting for performance they experience, love and praise doled out for achievement are still conditional. No wonder young people struggle to cope with perceived failure.

"Stupid people are dangerous"

Even seemingly respected researchers have some very limited explanations of youth anxiety. For example, Jean Twenge, Professor of Psychology at San Diego State University, one of the most prominent commentators on what's up with the kids, blames rising rates of depression on a decrease in social interaction due to social media. She even called one of her books *iGen*.

But Twenge isn't very interested in the economic and environmental reasons that explain why young people feel as they do. She dismisses the importance of the financial crisis because unemployment has since fallen. But what's more important are the profound changes in employment over the past few decades: low pay, contract work, outsourcing, the gig economy and the way in which fear is normalized in endless downsizing, reorganizations, monitoring and performance reviews. Even among the "winners" there's overwork, constant competition and the pressure to achieve and then maintain status.

We'll note the stress passed on by social media later. But when the world is catching fire around them, blaming young people's use of apps for an epidemic of mental illness doesn't add up. The shame agenda of commentators like Twenge is obvious from her book titles like *The Narcissism Epidemic* and *Generation Me*.

Such commentary can also be sexist. Most of the rise in supposed "narcissism" comes from girls and women, previous generations of whom have been taught that pride and confidence are unfeminine. Like many of them, Katniss lacks self-esteem at the start of *The Hunger Games*. But also like today's girls and young women, she will come to challenge those who seek to deny her a voice.

"I mean, what am I allowed to care about at this point?"

These characterizations of young people don't stem (just) from commentators being cranky olds. They serve as a distraction from an exploitative economic system, from austerity and insecurity, and ever-increasing psychological pressure for personal productivity and perfectionism generated by contemporary capitalism. And as we'll see, from coming collapse. No wonder people feel ill.

As Shoshana Zuboff (*The Age of Surveillance Capitalism*) identifies, the contradiction at the heart of our dominant economic ideology is that we are promised control over our own lives, but everywhere this is thwarted by inequality, exclusion, competition, and social and economic stratification. What's really being denied is that our economies no longer even seriously promise a better future, or even a relatively secure one.

In *Capitalist Realism,* Mark Fisher points to several ways in which capitalism is detrimental to our mental wellbeing, including job insecurity, the toll of overwork on families, the envy and inadequacy stoked by advertising, financial hardship and its equation with personal failure. We need to ask how it's become acceptable that so many people are so ill. Rather than being the only system that works, capitalism seems inherently dysfunctional to human wellbeing. As Mark notes, denying the social causes of sickness leaves us to suffer and struggle alone. However useful they might be, the treatments offered, typically therapy and pharmaceuticals, are individualized. Healing and recovery are rarely collective, let alone political or economic.

As Jennifer Silva argues in *Coming Up Short: Working-Class Adulthood in an Age of Uncertainty,* millennials (especially working-class young people) are alienated. The American Dream, the national myth, has failed, preventing many of them from reaching former markers of adulthood. In an economy that puts stable employment and home ownership out of reach, young people have embraced a "therapeutic model of selfhood" built on self-sufficiency and overcoming personal trauma.

Silva draws on Sennett and Cobb in recognizing that when the system seems unchangeable, we're forced to think about transformation only in individual terms. Rather than turning to politics to restore hope and dignity, many young people try to build meaning and identity through the struggle to exorcise the demons of familial abuse, mental health problems, addiction or betrayal in past relationships.

To Silva, this dramatic but largely unnoticed shift reduces becoming an adult to solitary suffering, self-blame and an endless seeking for signs of progress. The self, rather than society, comes to be regarded as the greatest obstacle to success. Worst of all, the system teaches young people to be distrustful of interdependence and solidarity with others, as if these are weaknesses rather than the only real solution to their problems, to our problems.

As Alice Miller (*Banished Knowledge: Facing Childhood Injuries*) argues, this internalization stems from trying to avoid feeling the full pain of victimhood: "[I]t is easier to see oneself as a criminal than to know and feel that one was, and is, an innocent victim who must be prepared at all times for torture and persecution. Every patient clings to fantasies in which he sees himself in the active role so as to escape the pain of being defenseless and helpless."

So of course young people identify with Katniss, whose only markers of adulthood are accepting responsibility for her family's survival and being thrown into a brutally competitive arena in which she'll struggle to survive.

"Whatever the opposite of fine is, that's what I am"

Economist Noreena Hertz has called those born between 1995-2002 "Generation K," after Katniss. This is a generation riddled with anxiety and distrustful of traditional institutions, but like their heroine also imbued with a strong sense of social justice.

They look out on a world of terror and insecurity. Of course they've been shaped by technology and recession, but also by existential threat. As Hertz says: "[U]nlike those currently aged between 20 and 30, the 'Yes we can' generation, who grew up believing the world was their oyster, for Generation K the world is less oyster, more Hobbesian nightmare." Rather than shaming them, Hertz's research with 2000 American and British teenagers suggests they're defined by anxiety, loneliness and fear about their own futures as well as the world – but also by a distrust of corporations, a desire for connection and co-creation, and a commitment to equality and the environment.

In the absence of such explanations, generational monikers are used to try to discredit an intelligent, hard-working, low-earning, socially conscious but fed-up generation trying to survive a gathering crisis of capitalism, state and corporate corruption, police brutality and resurgent hate crime. If they dare to call for change, they're characterized as indulging in adolescent tantrums or mounting a manevolent movement against free speech. These are all attempts at containment, of course, to dismiss, distract, mischaracterize and mock their calls for justice. It's the Capitol's marginalization of any criticism that makes us hold our tongues, just like Katniss does.

Also like Katniss, given the state of the world, as many as 30 percent of teenage girls either don't want to get married or are unsure. Even more strikingly, 35 percent don't know if they want to have children or definitely don't, a major change compared to older millennials.

As Sara Ahmed (*Promise of Happiness*) suggests, feeling that the world is odd means feeling at odds with the world. We're no longer well adjusted, because we can't adjust to *this* world.

"Something inside me shuts down and I'm too numb to feel anything"

There's a lot not to adjust to. Cruelty and violence permeates *The Hunger Games* of course. The Games themselves are just the pinnacle of the Capitol's physical and institutional violence against most of the people of Panem (we'll enter the Games' arena in Chapter 5). But in our world, cruelty and violence have also become familiar ways of lashing out, expressing fear, pain and dysfunction.

The US is a particularly fear-based society, economically, socially, politically, culturally, psychologically. There's the obvious trauma from a physically violent society, in gun violence, school shootings, racial attacks, police abuse and the media's sensational packaging of it all. But as in Panem, these are just the most obvious manifestations of a deeper culture of fear.

According to the annual Chapman University Survey of American Fears, Americans are more afraid than ever. Its 2018 survey revealed that government corruption remains Americans' primary concern. More than half of Americans fear not having enough money for the future and people close to them becoming seriously ill (with, of course, extortionate medical bills). But for the first time in this survey, the environment comprises half of Americans' top ten fears (not one environmental concern made the list in 2016) – from the pollution of oceans, rivers and lakes, and drinking water, to air pollution, the extinction of plant and animal species, and climate change.

In such an atmosphere we become numbed, in mental ill health and substance addiction. Another reason for the generational resonance of *The Hunger Games* is that it takes seriously the lasting trauma on its young people of competition and cruelty, first from the system under which they try to survive, then in the Games and finally in the armed rebellion against the elite. It asks, what are the costs of all this conflict, and how is it possible to cope?

"Poison. The perfect weapon for a snake"

There's a lot of projection in elders' descriptions of young people. In *The Hunger Games*, as embodied in the Capitol, it's the adults who are frivolous, vacuous, narcissistic, hedonistic, entitled, swayed by melodrama and sentimental emotion. Meanwhile, the young people in the districts act for each other and their families. Throughout, Katniss always tries to behave responsibly, agonizes over how to avoid further violence, tries to consider what's the best choice in every moment, but also the longer-term consequences of her decisions.

So it is in our world that the generational "debate" is an inversion of reality. It's hardly frivolous to be fearful of a future of rising seas, burning forests and drought-ridden crop land (discussed in the next chapter). The ultimate narcissism is not to care because you'll be long dead by then.

But Suzanne Collins also makes a broader point. The regime

sickens everyone: residents of the districts, rebels, tributes, but also the victors and residents of the Capitol, with their gluttony, inanity, plastic surgery and addictions. Even President Snow, poisoned and bleeding from his many crimes, and before him, Seneca the Gamemaker too, given no choice but to eat deadly berries after he's outwitted by events. As James Baldwin remarked, "People who treat other people as less than human must not be surprised when the bread they have cast on the waters comes floating back to them, poisoned."

"Because that's what you and I do, protect each other"

Although they might seem similar, the antithesis of *The Hunger Games* is William Golding's *Lord of the Flies*. It encapsulates the adult fear of the brutality of teenagers, that left to their own devices, they inevitably descend into a state of selfish brutality. But it's projection, a rationalization to justify containing young people. Instead, Panem has to construct its state of selfish brutality.

As Judith Rich Harris argues in *The Nurture Assumption*, psychologists and parents have long believed that they matter to teenagers' development, as of course they would. In fact, Harris suggests, evolution has endowed teenagers with enough imagination, resilience and empathy to survive in the world as long as they have each other. What really matters to their social, intellectual and emotional development is being given the space to develop and maintain a close circle of friends.

And yet, as noted, for a variety of reasons children are being given less time to be children and to associate with their peers. In fact, reflecting the *Lord of the Flies*, modern day parents seem to have developed a pervasive paranoia about protecting their child from other children.

"They messed us up pretty good, didn't they?"

"It's all a big show. It's all how you're perceived"

By design, the Hunger Games commodify the competitors, turning them into objects, always a precondition for abuse and exploitation, so that the audience can be entertained rather than horrified by their suffering.

Leading up to the Games, the tributes are expected to act cheerfully and hide just how afraid they are. Katniss and Peeta and all of the other tributes are taken to the "Remake Center." Katniss is literally scrubbed clean of the scars of her life in District 12. They're styled for a grand parade, then have to pitch themselves on a confessional-style talkshow. Each tribute is treated as a character, distinct from the human being who is about to kill or, more likely, be killed. The audience doesn't experience them as real people, which might induce empathy with their plight. This also goes for the young people kidnapped for the Games; the more they see the other tributes only as competition, the easier it will be to murder them and win the "prize," which is to say, survive.

Katniss has to pretend she's humbled, awed, to be in the Games, "this little girl from District Twelve." She has to compliment the Capitol, literally pay tribute to it. Even in the arena, the competitors have to consider how to solicit crucial supplies from rich "sponsors" in the Capitol (as Haymitch advises Katniss, "You really wanna know how to stay alive? You get people to like you"). Just before being thrown into the arena, the tributes are given a rating by the Gamemakers based on their chances of survival, which is important to attracting sponsors. Obviously, because no one wants to back a loser.

The more Katniss seems appealing, charming, sympathetic and somehow a willing participant in the Games, the more sponsors she stands a chance of attracting. There's an echo here of what sociologist Arlie Hochschild in her 1983 book *The Managed Heart* called emotional labor, the suppression and evoking of certain feelings demanded by work, often in low-paid service jobs. And after the trauma of the arena, Katniss is cleaned up for the post-Games interview, as if the horror never happened.

Most obviously, during the Games, Katniss wrestles with Peeta's apparent love for her. At times she reasons that he's just playing for the cameras, for the Capitol audience, at other times she's genuinely confused about why anyone would desire her. Again, she's internalized the falseness of the Capitol's media constructions, assuming that his emotions aren't real.

"Together? Together"

Suzanne Collins' most obvious inspiration is reality TV. She's explained that: "I was channel surfing between reality TV programing and actual war coverage when Katniss's story came to me. One night I'm sitting there flipping around and on one channel there's a group of young people competing for, I don't know, money maybe? And on the next there's a group of young people fighting an actual war. And I was tired, and the lines began to blur in this very unsettling way..."

We'll return to reality television in Chapter 5, when we examine the Games in more detail. But for the moment, Collins captures how contemporary capitalism creates pressure for young people to commodify themselves, to craft a personal brand, perform, and promote their "best" identity. Of course, social media provides the perfect vehicle for this. As Jia Tolento argues in *Trick Mirror*, these platforms are all about commodifying selfhood, but are leading us to mass alienation. Social media offers a kind of ameliorative solidarity which isn't real; we gravitate to social media in order to feel more connected, but often feel more isolated (later, we consider actual, radical solidarity).

It's just one respect in which *The Hunger Games* is less sci-fi dystopia than current critique. Many of the twentieth century's most famous fictional dystopias are about the individual being crushed under the heel of a totalitarian state (*Nineteen Eighty-Four, Brave New World, Fahrenheit 451, Atlas Shrugged* from the libertarian right). But Collins' dark vision is different. The torture of the Games is more about consumerism than the collective – it's constructed "entertainment," but a distraction with a design, to divide us. Instead, as we'll suggest later, the solution lies in the collective, in people coming together.

"I try to remember who I am and who I am not"

The danger of course is that all of this role playing risks us losing a sense of who we are. In *Catching Fire*, the second book/film in the series, Katniss realizes to her horror that she must continue the story that she and Peeta are in love, for their survival and that of their families. Although she lived in poverty in District 12, at least she had the freedom to marry who she wanted. Now even that's been taken from her. (Perhaps the most insidious example of the regime's exploitation of young people is how Finnick, a former winner of the Games, is forced by President Snow into prostitution for the Capitol elite.)

Later, in *Mockingjay*, the third in the series, Katniss is used as a symbol by the revolution, but she's deeply conflicted about adopting this persona, both about her ability to play the role effectively, and the consequences of the conflict with the Capitol.

Contrary to his hope before the Games about retaining his integrity, Peeta's identity is scrambled by the Capitol under torture (the rebels call it "hijacking"), conditioned against his true feelings to hate Katniss. For Katniss, in a mirror of Peeta's predicament, her identity has been hijacked by the rebels. As she thinks, "Why am I hopping around like some trained dog trying to please people I hate?" She comes to feel as if she is "no one at all." (Most powerfully, at a crucial point in the story, Katniss will decide that the only way out is to end the self completely.)

But as noted, perhaps the most insidious, often invisible erosion of the self derives from the daily grinding focus on survival, a kind of identity theft by a cruel, corrupt society. Katniss' struggle will be to recognize who she really is, something that totalitarian regimes never encourage, since the beginning of the true self is often the beginning of the end of tyranny.

"They're afraid of you"

Why does the Capitol go to all of this trouble to treat "its" young people so horrendously, at the risk of generating widespread disgust at its rule? Because its fear of them is even greater.

The Capitol tries to contain its children because it's terrified of them politically, because despite its propaganda, there's nothing natural about the state it's created and coerces people into accepting. Its fear of youth is really its fear of how they could challenge its institutions of exploitation. In Panem, the Games are a pre-emptive punishment against young people's revolutionary potential.

What *The Hunger Games* points to, an important part of its success with young readers, is its examination of how youth oppression is so normalized that we often don't notice it. Children are considered property. Their "owners" (parents/guardians) have rights over them. Children and young people are indoctrinated into submission and subservience by schools, churches, the police, legal systems, as well as in the home. They are regularly ignored, neglected, compelled and brutalized. As an insurance policy, at the earliest possible age these institutions stunt self-confidence, individuality and creativity, knowing that this makes their resurgence in later life much less likely.

Hobbesians would argue that, without adult indoctrination, children would naturally develop classism, sexism, authoritarianism and racism of their own accord. It seems much more likely that they'd instinctively recognize that power should be shared equally between individuals and groups. We're born anarchists; we need to be taught irrational oppressions. If the corruption of adults begins with the corruption of children, we need a revolution in nurturing.

As argued by the authors of *Liberating Youth*, a radical pamphlet, youthism – the rejection of indoctrination and social engineering, replaced by liberty for young people founded on free association – is arguably the most neglected of our liberation struggles. Until it's realized, the adult world, as a matter of its own survival, must break young people lest they break it. Much like the Capitol knows it must break its young people if its regime is to persist.

"You could do a lot worse, you know"

A powerful way that political authorities establish and reinforce their dominance is to implicitly and explicitly present themselves as the wise but distant disciplining parent, especially the father figure. President Snow sits at the head of the national family – mean, unsmiling and remote.

Alice Miller was among those who made an important link between abuse experienced in childhood and political authoritarianism, via the rationalization of violence to dominate and control others. Cruelty to children, and the denial and repression of these emotions, breeds adults' acceptance of totalitarianism, and of course fascism glorifies violence and domination.

To Miller, the abused child must repress the mistreatment and neglect she suffered, otherwise the pain would be too great to bear. But what was once life-saving can in adulthood turn into a dangerous, destructive ideology. As she wrote (*Breaking Down the Wall of Silence*):

> To sign away our democratic rights to future tyrants and dictators, because they cast themselves in the role of "strong fathers," thus reminding us of our own, is tantamount to committing collective suicide. Even if we have, since childhood, been waiting for the great, redeeming figure who

will solve all our problems, as adults we can be aware that such a redeemer will, in reality, turn out to be something quite different.

The lives of dictators support Miller's argument that they prefer to see thousands, even millions, of people killed and tortured rather than face their childhood mistreatment, to ever feel again the humiliation and helplessness they once felt from their parents, let alone to call them to account for their actions. Hence then the ideologies of domination they promote to legitimize punishment and coercion "for your own good," echoing Hobbes of course.

A particularly important aspect of these ideologies is to despise what they regard as weakness, helplessness, or uncertainty (natural characteristics in children of course). Instead, they admire projections of strength, grandiosity and absolute belief. We see these characteristics in the Capitol, just as we see them in the authoritarian populists of our own world.

The problem is when we accept their "values" as our own, when we come to despise the poor, or ourselves, for our fears and insecurities or lack of wealth and status. By now, you'll have anticipated that Katniss embodies some of these complexes, and she does. But we can take hope from the depiction found in *The Hunger Games*. The residents of the districts aren't constantly dehumanizing each other; it takes the Capitol's costly artifice of the Games to promote the pretense that they are. Similarly, in our experience so many despised poor and marginalized communities don't take on the economic, social, cultural, political violence that's been done to them. They're better than the Capitol.

"Crying is not an option"

Adults should protect young people, not punish them. But protective adults are too often absent. The activist and organizer

Andrew Slack has noted the prevalence of "orphans versus empires" in much popular fantasy, from Dorothy in the *Wizard of Oz*, and *Superman* and many other superheroes, to *Harry Potter*. As Andrew suggests, this isn't a coincidence.

Orphanhood is also reflected in *The Hunger Games*. Katniss and Prim have lost their father and effectively their mother as well. Katniss is angry about her mother, even though she can understand it. Like many children from dysfunctional homes, Katniss keeps their situation secret from the outside world, out of fear of the authorities taking her and her sister away into "care." The other young people don't really seem to have present parents either. And then, being taken from their homes and forced to fight in the Games represents the ultimate orphanhood.

But politically as well, as young people push further into the world, they discover another orphanhood. There is no real adult leadership, responsibility or nurturing in Panem. And not enough in our world either. Young people are orphans of a system that has abandoned them, and humanity. Like Katniss, they're a generation left to figure it out for themselves.

"As long as you can find yourself, you'll never starve"

Brutal competition, the stark division between winners and losers, constant surveillence, the pressure of perfomative living, the fear that life might be over before it's really begun...of course *The Hunger Games* speaks to young people. In its dramatization of ordinary young heroes fighting for their lives, and to retain their dignity and integrity, they see their world and who they might have to be in it.

The Capitol and its commentators want them to submit to its propaganda, to doubt their own senses, and to blame themselves for failing to fit into its fraudulent constructions. But the reality of the system is revealed in what they feel and experience: fear, anxiety, trauma, alienation, hopelessness.

It takes Katniss a long time to recognize that her power lies in her fragility, vulnerability and flaws – in her humanity ("The damage, the fatigue, the imperfections. That's how they recognize me, why I belong to them"). Alice Miller once wrote that, "Our capacity to resist has nothing to do with our intelligence but with the degree of access to our true self." Against the odds, it's the true self that we need to protect under the present capitalism and in the coming collapse. Every day we stay alive, and stay well, is an act of rebellion.

Oh, and it turns out that the elders in the Capitol are right to fear the young people of Panem.

Chapter 3

"Look at the state they left us in"

"Tick tock"

It's little commented on, but *The Hunger Games* is about civilizational collapse. In the books, before the reaping, the mayor of District 12 recounts the history of Panem, "...the disasters, the droughts, the storms, the fires, the encroaching seas that swallowed up so much of the land, the brutal war for what little sustenance remained" (the backstory of environmental disaster is not mentioned in the films). There's also a later reference to "the destruction of the atmosphere." Panem is post-collapse. It's also our future.

We don't know exactly when, but we do know that the original trilogy is set more than a hundred years in the future. There's a comment that District 13 is the "work of centuries," though this probably refers to some of its underground complex being built much earlier, in our time or even before. Even in advance of the prequel *The Ballad of Songbirds and Snakes*, there's a lot we can say about how, in our world, as a result of environmental, economic, social and political crises, the most likely outcome is an authoritarian regime not unlike that described in the series.

Climate change and environmental destruction will lead to failing food production systems, widespread hunger, more conflict and refugees, greater social control and ultimately authoritarianism. Crisis will provide the opportunity for elites to establish new regimes built on segregation and exploitation. We're already living in an early collapse politics which is increasingly divisive and autocratic. There's much more to come.

Collapse also helps to explain young people's trauma; they know (some of) what's coming and have a sense of hopelessnes, fear and frustration. Some young people are fighting back, setting the stage for a generational war. Unfortunately, it's one they're likely to lose.

The Hunger Games isn't speculative science fiction. There's no new technology here that we haven't seen in many other future-set stories. The series is speculative political science, a warning that's coming true. The future is already in our present. The world is catching fire.

"Welcome to the new Panem"

We have no definitive guide to what will happen and when. But it's inevitable, not a single problem we can avoid or engineer our way out of, but a civilizational predicament we're locked into and which it's too late to avoid. The roots of our crisis lie in an unfair, unequal, unsustainable, fossil fuel-dependent economic system, and the attempts to defend it which are using authoritarianism and populist politics as a distraction.

In the world of *The Hunger Games,* environmental crisis destroyed the United States' economy and agriculture. This resulted in a civil war over scarce food supplies, culminating in a totalitarian regime. But the districts rebelled against the Capitol. Hunger and conflict nearly killed off the whole of humankind, or at least the population of the former United States. The districts lost, leaving a highly segregated, autocratic society of poverty and backwardness for a majority, and extreme wealth and advanced technology for a protected few.

This background is clearly important to Suzanne Collins. She's said:

> It's crucial that young readers are considering scenarios about humanity's future, because the challenges are about to land in their laps. In *The Hunger Games* I hope they question how elements of the books might be relevant to their own lives. About global warming, about our mistreatment of the environment, but also questions like: How do you feel about

the fact that some people take their next meal for granted when so many other people are starving in the world?

"I haven't realized it 'til now, but I've been dead all along, haven't I?"

Young people are considering humanity's future. It's another reason why they're fearful.

The youngest generation have really only known early collapse: terror, war, economic crisis, social division, political instability and the rise of authoritarian populism. No one under 30 has known a stable climate. Not a single month in their lifetime has fallen within the temperature range, rain or storm activity that has governed the planet for the past 10,000 years. Successive generations will grow up into a world shaped entirely by collapse, forced to compete in a hunger games of their own.

At the same time, under capitalism, young people have been stripped of the possibility of change, even though they fear we face the end of civilization. This is crucial to understanding their worsening mental health. Of course they're anxious, worried, distressed. Like Katniss, they live under gathering clouds and grim uncertainty, unable to envisage a different future.

According to the American Psychological Association, 58 percent of American Gen Zers cite climate change as a significant source of stress; mass shootings, rising rates of suicide, the separation and deportation of migrant families, and sexual assault and harrassment are also major worries. More than two-thirds say they feel very or somewhat significantly stressed about America's future. For more than three in 10, personal debt and housing instability also cause significant anxiety, while nearly the same amount cite hunger and getting enough to eat.

Globally, Amnesty International's *Future of Humanity* survey confirms that young people see climate change as the most important issue facing the world. Nationally, young people also cite corruption, economic instability, pollution and income inequality as the most pressing problems.

If you're young, you're going to witness the destabilization of life on earth: massive crop failures, apocalyptic fires, imploding economies, widespread flooding and hundreds of millions of refugees fleeing regions made uninhabitable by extreme heat and permanent drought. Studies show that the fear of nuclear-annihilation scarred children growing up in the Cold War. Gen Z is already scarred by their equivalent. Many young people think that they'll die from climate change before they die of old age. It's the reaping hanging over them.

"The disasters, the droughts, the storms, the fires"

Climate change, let alone collapse, often seems too abstract for many people to think about. Popular culture has been one way of trying to bring home the effects, but at the risk of misleading dramatic depictions that distance people from what's going to happen, or induce despair rather than motivate them to take action. The scenario in *The Hunger Games* is a better way to describe what's most likely, something everyone can relate to: food.

Globally, industry and agriculture combined consume 88 percent of all the water we use (69 percent by agriculture, 19 percent by industry). Severe droughts will seriously impact both. By 2050, as much as 30 percent of the world's land surface could face desert-like conditions, including large swaths of Asia, Europe, Africa and southern Australia. More than 1.5 billion people currently live in these regions.

Droughts, floods, storms and massive disruption brought by climate change will increasingly threaten global food supplies from the 2020s. This will happen even if we're able to keep global temprature rises to 1.5°C (the goal of the 2016 Paris climate change agreement). The food system, which already fails to feed many people, won't be able to cope if global heating surges beyond 2°C. But at current rates of carbon emissions, we're on course for a truly disastrous 3°C of heating.

"The encroaching seas that swallowed up so much of the land"

In rich Western countries, we often think of climate change as something that will mainly happen to "people far away," and it's true that the poorest and most vulnerable people face the greatest destruction. But we won't be as insulated as we assume.

James Hansen, probably the most respected climate scientist in the world, has warned that we face losing most of the world's large coastal cities, not hundreds of years from now but this century. As he puts it, "If we don't demand radical change we are headed for a whole world of people searching for a home that no longer exists."

Rising seas could affect three times more people by 2050 than previously thought, erasing some of the world's major cities: Bangkok, Mumbai, Shanghai, Ho Chi Minh City...150 million people live on land that will be below high tide by the middle of this century. And this is the "hopeful" scenario, where warming is held to 2°C and the ice sheets don't collapse. In the more pessimistic scenario, this doubles to 300 million people flooded by 2050 – approaching the total population of the United States.

Climate change will reshape America as well. By the end of the century, 80 million Americans could be forced to flee the coasts. Rising seas will mean mass relocation from some areas, but this raises huge concerns about justice. There's a pernicious history of forced movement of people of color, from slavery, the treatment of Native Americans, Japanese internment camps, to slum clearance, "urban renewal" and redlining. This could all happen again.

Or people will just be left to drown. The cost of building sea walls to protect US coastal cities is predicted to reach $400 billion by 2040. Which is highly unlikely to happen; government is much more likely to protect richer people first, or only (federal government buyouts of homes in flood-prone areas are already biased toward the rich). It's easy to imagine the Capitol sacrificing poorer areas and securing itself.

Solomon Hsiang of the University of California, Berkeley, predicts (with co-researcher Amir Jina) that as the climate heats up there will be a large transfer of wealth northward and westward; in *The Hunger Games* this reflects the location of Panem's Capitol west of the Rocky Mountains, on higher ground. Hsiang suggests this could result in the largest transfer of wealth from the poor to the rich in American history. The latter, who can afford to adapt, might even benefit, while the former will be left behind. The Southeast will be the biggest loser from flooding, heat mortality and lower agricultural yields.

"The brutal war for what little sustenance remained"

The climate crisis is damaging the ability of land to sustain us, with cascading risks as temperatures rise. Global heating is increasing droughts, soil erosion and wildfires, and diminishing crop yields. Crops have already failed in many places over the last 5 years, including North and Central Africa, the Middle East, India, Pakistan, northern China, northern Europe, Argentina, Brazil, Central America and even parts of North America.

Warming of 2°C, which we could hit by the end of the 2020s, will mean droughts lasting longer than 3 months that are more than twice as severe compared to the 1990s, desertification affecting most of the world's soil, a huge increase in crop-destroying pests and a massive decline in the viability of the crops that are critical for human survival. Even passing 1.5 °C could trigger major production losses of millions of tonnes of maize, wheat and soybean. Pest-related yield losses from wheat, rice and maize are predicted to increase by 46 percent, 19 percent and 31 percent respectively.

Consequently, the climate crisis will lead to the collapse of some poorer countries' economies which are dependent on cash crops, grown primarily for export to world markets.

Hunger triggers conflict, which in turn causes more hunger. As the effects of climate change have increased, state-based conflict has risen by 60 percent since 2010 and armed conflict within countries by 125 percent. Between 2015-2019, there have been more state-based conflicts than at any time since the Second World War, with an estimated 1 million deaths. And according to the Food and Agriculture Organization of the United Nations, more than half of food-insecure people (489 million out of 815 million) live in countries experiencing violence. More than three-quarters of the world's chronically malnourished children (122 million of 155 million) live in conflict regions.

Conflict hits farmers especially hard. It evicts them from their land, destroys crops and livestock, prevents them from selling their produce, and disrupts planting and harvesting. Conflict-torn communities become more vulnerable to climate-related disaster. This causes more migration and refugees. The number of refugees and internally displaced persons doubled between 2007 and 2016. Of the 64 million people currently displaced, more than 15 million are related to the most severe conflict-related food crises in Syria, Yemen, Iraq, South Sudan, Nigeria and Somalia. In the years before 2011, global food price spikes linked to climate breakdown helped to trigger the Arab Spring uprisings.

Western countries are not imune. For example, agricultural failures in Syria drove mass migrations, forcing an immense number of farmers (maybe a million farm families) off their land and into the cities. This left large numbers of people, especially young men, unemployed, desperate and discontent. Many flooded into cities, overwhelming limited resources and services, and exacerbating existing sectarian tensions that sparked a protracted civil war. In turn, many people tried to flee to the rest of the world. Inside of 18 months they threw the politics of Western Europe into a deeper spiral of discontent; refugees were used by populist authoritarians to call for anti-immigrant and more insular policies.

Take this effect and multiply it by hundreds. This is our future.

"Anyone could see the game was over at that point"

As Umair Haque (*The Age of Collapse*) has put it, neoliberalism – the particularly aggressive form of capitalism promoted over the past 40 years – is fundamentally based on extraction. In Chapter 1, we saw how this has shaped regions such as Appalachia. It's also why we face a civilizational crisis:

> Collapse of this kind means that we are undernourishing and impoverishing the weakest things around us. We are "overconsuming" them, in economic terms, and, conversely, "underinvesting" in them. Whether it's insects, bees, glaciers, decent jobs, or social contracts – we seem to be rampaging through all the things that are the most defenseless of all, until there is nothing of them left. But that is exactly what capitalism and neoliberalism say we should do.

We wonder how elites don't see it. But they're not in denial. For them, it isn't capitalism that will collapse, it's democracy, into full oligarchy. A Panem-like society isn't the accidental outcome of this ideology, it's the inevitable, and desired, endgame.

It started with neoliberalism. This suppressed workers' wages, deregulated banks and gave huge tax breaks to corporations and the rich. Ever since, wealth has been redistributed upwards to elites, taking us toward oligarchy, rule by the wealthy (as we'll see in the next chapter, the Capitol and the districts represent the capitalist class system laid bare). And now, with climate change, it will get much, much worse.

But elites aren't stupid. They understand the data and see the effects. Oil companies and others have known about climate change for decades. But they're not going to give up on a system that has ensured them such enormous wealth and power.

As the saying goes, it's easier to envisage the end of the world than the end of capitalism. But for elites, the former doesn't mean the latter. Power and wealth was all they really wanted anyway. As we burn, they have no intention of burning with us.

When they can't deny the crisis any longer, they'll blame it on "human nature," on the inherent greed and short-sightedness of our species. But this is just an echo of the Hobbesian argument that we're naturally selfish, or even that there are simply too many of us, so expect the emergence of ecofascism.

In truth, it's the system that's the cause of the crisis. As Naomi Klein ("Let Them Drown") argues, it's:

> Capitalism, colonialism, patriarchy – those sorts of system. Diagnoses like this erase the very existence of human systems that organised life differently: systems that insist that humans must think seven generations in the future; must be not only good citizens but also good ancestors; must take no more than they need and give back to the land in order to protect and augment the cycles of regeneration. These systems existed and still exist, but they are erased every time we say that the climate crisis is a crisis of "human nature" and that we are living in the "age of man."

"We're facing an enemy that will not change"

As collapse becomes unavoidable, the open secret of elites' endgame becomes clear: a destroyed environment, fortress enclaves for the rich, segregated exploitation for the rest of us.

As the technologist Vinay Gupta suggests, historically, the response to increasing scarcity (economic inequality, poverty, rising prices) is the centralization of power (and ultimately, fascism). Capitalism in crisis has often allied with authoritarianism. The destruction and instability wrought by climate change takes the "ordinary" periodic crises of capitalism to an existential, civilizational level.

The new authoritarians can see the huge opportunity in collapse: their chance to finish the job, a more extreme version of the world that already exists, where inequality strangles democracy, austerity is a weapon of class war, millions die from pollution and environmental destruction, conflict escalates, surveillance and incarceration increases, and corporations rule.

We've seen how the shock doctrine operates, how disaster capitalism seizes on natural events, like floods or man-made political crises, to advance and entrench elite and corporate power. The utlimate, combined crisis of climate change, the collapse of everyday essentials such as the food production system, and economic destablization – what David Wallace-Wells calls in *The Uninhabitable Earth* the "Great Dying" – will likely lead to a form of techno-fascism. Authoritarian state capitalism will be strengthened, advanced technology will be in the hands of elites, and there will be scarcity and harshness beyond the safe walls of the Capitol.

As Fabian Scheidler (*The End of the Megamachine*) suggests, in the absence of any real transition plan:

> [G]lobal elites fence themselves in high-security gated communities and seem determined to defend their privileges by all means. A fight for the pockets of affluence seems to be on the horizon, and in many countries authoritarian, fundamentalist and racist forces are ascending. Because a transitional plan is lacking we have to anticipate ever more dramatic systemic breakdowns: financial crashes, ecological disasters and social crises.

"And then I understand. The Games are still on"

Peter Frase similarly sketches this as the most likely of the *Four Futures: Life After Capitalism* we face – a dystopia in which the rich retreat to fortified compounds while the rest of us are trapped outside, drowning in the hell of a rapidly warming planet. It's a world of compounds, camps, walls and fences. As Frase suggests, the endgame is not to save civilization but a capitalist order that protects and privileges the wealthy and powerful.

Actually, there will be two futures happening at the same time. The elite will effectively be living in the future, the rest of us will be marooned in the past. This is depicted in *The Hunger Games* as well. As Mark Fisher ("Precarious Dystopias") notes:

> ...the Capitol's decadent (post)modernity, its apparently unlimited consumption and foppish, infantilised spectatorialism can be set against the conspicuous authenticity of older forms of labour, with their dirt poor privations and honest work ethic. When Katniss, the daughter of a dead miner who survives by hunting on the land, is conveyed to the Capitol by high-speed train, it is as if the nineteenth century is brought face to future-shocked face with twenty-first century media culture.

The cyberpunk author William Gibson famously remarked that, "The future is already here, it's just not evenly distributed," by which he meant who gets to play with technological advancements. But as Vinay Gupta ("Waking Up in the Monster Factory") reminds us, the same goes for collapse:

> It's not that "collapse" is happening – what you call "poverty" is collapse. All those homeless people, that's collapse; all those people dying without health insurance, that's collapse; all those people who are addicted to opiates because their doctors will write them a prescription and their health insurance will provide them with a drug which will kill them, that is collapse. The thing about collapse is it's not until it happens to you or your immediate family or your

very closest friends that you recognize it as collapse – up until then it's just economics. The collapse is already here, it's just not evenly distributed.

"We'll turn their advance into a celebration of suffering"

Climate change isn't just about things getting hotter and wetter, it's about things getting meaner and uglier. As Naomi Klein ("Let Them Drown") has said, we're seeing the beginning of an era of climate barbarism:

> [T]he same capacity for dehumanising the other that justified the bombs and drones is now being trained on these [conflict and climate] migrants, casting their need for security as a threat to ours, their desperate flight as some sort of invading army…A culture that places so little value on black and brown lives that it is willing to let human beings disappear beneath the waves, or set themselves on fire in detention centres, will also be willing to let the countries where black and brown people live disappear beneath the waves, or desiccate in the arid heat. When that happens, theories of human hierarchy – that we must take care of our own first – will be marshalled to rationalise these monstrous decisions. We are making this rationalisation already, if only implicitly.

Cory Doctorow has stated darkly that: "Climate denial has always been a function of greed, and where there is greed, genocide is always lurking in the shadows." The climate and environmental justice movement has long recognized that authoritarianism, racism and hierarchy are connected. As the young climate activist Jamie Margolin among others has articulated, behind the denial or acquiescence about climate change is a white supremacist ideology of separation ("We were already over 350ppm when I was born", *The Guardian*, July 12, 2019):

> [The] Same imperialist and supremacist mentality: Colonialism's mindset of heedless extraction, greed and human exploitation not only planted the seeds of today's climate crisis, it remains visible in the crisis's central injustice: although the poor are responsible for only a tiny share of humanity's greenhouse gas emissions, they generally suffer first and worst from the heatwaves, droughts, storms, rising seas and other effects of those emissions.

It's the same forever war there's always been. As Rebecca Solnit has put it in relation to gun violence, but also much more broadly ("Our forever war: how the white male hegemony uses violence to cling to power", *The Guardian*, 8 August 2019):

> We were never not at war, but in recent years the cold civil war has heated up. The white men who expected unquestioned supremacy...have launched a civil war against the rest of us, not least by allowing a huge number of high-capacity weapons of war to circulate throughout the country...The Republican party has in essence declared war against the United States – against the people, the environment, the constitution, the rule of law, against voting rights and free and fair elections. The threats are coming from inside the Capitol.

"So now that we're dead, what're we gonna do?"

The Hunger Games is about the coming collapse of America in particular (we don't hear about what happened to the rest of the world): its Roman-style imperial overreach, self-regard, decadence, lack of popular consent, hypocrisy and bankruptcy. It also represents a generational war: the elder-run regime that contains, exploits and punishes its children. The right has signed a death warrant, effectively a Treaty of Treason, for young people, the most vulnerable, the marginalized and disenfranchised.

In many Western countries, older elites have been ransacking the state for money, and piling up government debt and other obligations. As a result, we simply don't have enough money to recover from another financial crash, let alone solve the coming multiple crises. With climate change and collapse, many of them have chosen the Capitol over their own children.

Malcolm Harris (*Kids These Days*) argues that millennials (but it equally applies to Gen Zers) will either become "the first generation of true American fascists" or "the first generation of successful American revolutionaries."

It seems likely that some, the more privileged, will defend the system against the rest. Some will give up, lose themselves in distractions and addictions, or collapse into hopelessness and nihilism. Perhaps, like parts of the 1960s/1970s generation, some will drop out, go back to the land.

A few will go into survival mode, but lone survivalism is unrealistic. As Suzanne Collins suggests, based on her research on wilderness survival, "Here's what I learned: you've got to be really good to survive out there for more than a few days..." The right loves this survivalist vision, it reflects their Hobbesian brutal war of all against all. But Katniss' experience of the Games, and her day-to-day experience of living in the districts, shows how traumatizing just trying to survive can be (as we'll suggest in Chapter 7, there's a better way to survive).

Some will be drawn to right-wing authoritarian nationalism, even neo-fascism. But some will organize, protest, take direct action to try to promote a serious response to the crises. Many already are, of course, for example the school climate strikes, the developing global youth climate movement, Extinction Rebellion and so on.

Though they remain dominant in many countries due to their support from older people and wealthy interests, conservative parties in many Western countries have largely lost the young (the alt-right notwithstanding). Repeated surveys show that young people have an increasingly positive view of socialism and a more critical view of capitalism – a response to the insecurity, precarity, inequality, exploitation, as well as the climate crisis. As a result, right-wing governments will need to characterize, castigate and contain young people. They're doing it already. The characterizations of young people as manevolent – hysterical, entitled, narcissistic, a threat to freedom – will be used to justify containing them, sometimes literally.

As conditions worsen, there will probably be some kind of generational rebellion. Frustrated by the lack of response to crisis, some young people will become more militant, even take violent action against a system that's doomed them. But like the first rebellion in *The Hunger Games*, against the overwhelming power of the Capitol this is likely to fail. Violent protest will be used to justify state repression, and then we're heading into the hunger games.

"My dear Miss Everdeen, make no mistake, the game is coming to its end"

Remember the deceptive story that the Capitol tells about Panem's history: "The result was Panem, a shining Capitol ringed by thirteen districts, which brought peace and prosperity to its citizens." In other words, the Capitol was *strengthened* by collapse.

Despite thinking of itself as absent of denial, the left is wholly unprepared for collapse. It makes more progress when people believe that progress is possible, that history has hope. Some on the left believe in an "accelerationist automated communism," that we can harness technology for a radically more egalitarian society – a Capitol to which everyone is invited. And we could. But such visions of the future are so much more difficult to persuade people of when they're pessimistic about the possibility of change, and scared about who's going to get a share of shrinking resources.

Much of the left is hanging onto a past that elites are already exploiting the end of. It's the authoritarian populists of the right who've benefited the most politically from early collapse. As it advances further, collapse will tear to pieces the left's desire to direct an essentially stable state to share wealth much more widely. Collapse is corroding social trust, tolerance, truth. Crisis and scarcity are being used to spread fear and scapegoating. The elite's endgame is working.

As Saral Sarkar (*Eco-Socialism or Eco-Capitalism?*) states: "Even a truly socialist industrial society would perish because of this crisis. Any socialist revolution won't happen before the present civilization ends in global chaos, various kinds of war, and destruction. In the ruins of the present-day civilization it might not at all be possible to build a sustainable and socialist society."

As our societies struggle to respond, people's despair and disengagement with "democracy" will continue to grow. Confidence in it has weakened across Western countries; this has increased political instability and made populaces more prey to demagogues and disinformation. More people will look to seemingly "strong leaders" and reject liberal principles in favor of promises of greater "security."

Unfortunately, because of early collapse, our age of conflict, anger, polarization and denial is the worst possible context in which to try to engineer a more rational future. The Capitol is winning collapse. It looks like the districts have already lost.

"Would you like to be in a real war?"

In the backstory to *The Hunger Games*, during the Dark Days, the war between the Capitol and the districts nearly wiped out humanity. At some point the districts were forced to surrender, perhaps to save whoever remained. An armistice was signed, resulting in the Treaty of Treason. Perhaps the ultimate advantage held by the Capitol is that it's happy for people to die to protect its dominant position in Panem. Just like elites in our world.

For the center-left, there will be no steady progress toward the perfect social democratic, let alone democratic socialist, order. For the radical left, there will be no universal global revolution. Once, we might have thought that if we want to live in a different world, this world has to end. Now, this world is going to end, but in totally inhospitable ways. The challenge is how we might survive, and maybe one day, begin to build different worlds.

"I think these Games are going to be different"

The political-economic system of Panem (discussed more in the next part), and the Games especially, contain and sacrifice young people. This reflects a political fear of their natural questioning of the system, their inherent sense of justice and fairness, and possibly their revolutionary threat.

During the Games, Katniss just wants to go home, to return to her old life, despite its hardship. But under collapse and totalitarianism, there will be no home for us to go back to. Ultimately, one day, we may reach some kind of post-capitalist, post-industrial society. But there will be collapse first. We're going to the hunger games, and we need to find ways to survive. The odds are not in our favor. But the battle against the Capitol is not over just yet.

Part II

The Games

Chapter 4

"Welcome to the Capitol"

"Knowing it and seeing it are two different things"

Katniss and Peeta are transported by train to the Capitol. They've never been to Panem's ruling city before, but despite having seen it on television, they're amazed by the magnificence of its glistening towers, the shiny cars that glide down its wide streets, and its oddly dressed people with bizarre hair and painted faces who've never missed a meal.

It's one thing to hear about vast differences in wealth and power, it's another to experience them for yourself. And the fictional world of Panem reflects our reality. Two-thirds of the world survives on less than $10,000 – not even 2 percent of global wealth. Meanwhile, just 26 people own more than half of the world's population. Apparently, the Capitol is home to 5.6 million people, meaning that, statistically, the fictional future Panem understates the extent of the inequality in our actual present.

So let's not get distracted by the Capitol's towers. We need to investigate its foundations, how elites establish and maintain power, and how they've built their Capitol in our world.

"Everything is about them, not the dying boys and girls in the arena"

The elites of Panem are self-absorbed, vain, greedy, gluttonous hedonists. As Rebecca Solnit puts it, the Capitol is an amalgamation of Fashion Week, Versailles and the KGB/CIA ("Welcome to the 2012 Hunger Games", *Guernica,* 1 May 2012). To Tony McKenna (*Art, Literature and Culture from a Marxist Perspective*), its residents dress like they're in the court of Louis IV, which they pretty much are.

Given rapidly increasing inequality in our world, we've returned to a golden age for the gilded class. The production design in *The Hunger Games* films reflects the historical allusions, the Depression-era District 12 compared to the decadent art deco Capitol city. It also reflects the natural entitlement of the Capitol. The districts are just there to serve their needs, if they're thought about at all. Apart from once a year, when the residents of the Capitol watch from their high towers as district children are sacrificed for their entertainment.

"Of course, the odds have not been very dependable of late"

The Capitol is known for fashion, food and media, much like our global cities (tellingly also called alpha or power cities): New York, London, Tokyo, Hong Kong...They're swollen by socially unproductive sectors (finance, advertising, marketing, PR), so different from the laboring districts. The Capitol is where you dream of finding fame and success. More likely, if you're from the districts, you don't stand much chance; these sectors are dominated by the sons and daughters of privilege.

As Joel Kotkin (*The New Class Conflict*) suggests, this reflects a new geography of class struggle, which pits a new elite – oligarchs, technocrats, bureaucrats, the creative class – against the middle and working class, as well as generationally between old and young. Many millennials, saddled with low incomes and high debts, are forced to leave because they can't afford to live within the walls of wealth. And outside the walls, this geography has increasingly turned former heartlands, anywhere outside the Capitol(s) really, into dislocated, declining districts, as Phil A. Neel describes in *Hinterland: America's New Landscape of Class and Conflict*.

In contrast to the Capitol elite, the people of the districts have been demoralized to the extent that they don't feel *enough* entitlement – to their own labor, food, shelter, security and dignity. In our world, the Capitol has eroded whatever used to support this proper sense of entitlement, structures of social solidarity such as trade unions, as well as dismantling welfare systems. In Panem, there's no social security in the districts – a right-wing libertarian dream we're also heading toward (we discuss libertarian reading of *The Hunger Games* later on). Don't expect the state to ensure you don't starve, as conservatives like to say.

"The problem is, I can't tell what's real anymore, and what's made up"

It's not inevitable, though. Historically, capitalism has always been an imposed, engineered system – a social order. The Hungarian-American political economist Karl Polyani's most famous work, *The Great Transformation* (originally titled Origins of the Cataclysm), published in 1944, shows how there was nothing natural about how capitalism came about. As Polyani put it, "laissez-faire was planned."

Polyani focused on how in nineteenth-century England the poor were severed from the land and stripped of their access to charitable local support. Unable to count on subsistence from local parishes as under the previous system, they lined up at the gates of the workhouse. "No government was needed to maintain this balance," Polanyi noted, "it was restored by the pangs of hunger on the one hand, the scarcity of food on the other."

But in our time, neoliberal economists have told a very different story, inventing elaborate theories to "prove" that capitalism is natural. They've been so successful that any attempts to limit the power of capital and corporations are said to interfere with "natural forces." So, let's examine how they've built the system that provides them with such privilege.

"They're no better than the Capitol"

The Capitol elite aren't great entrepreneurs, bold visionaries, ground-breaking scientists, Panem's pioneers. It's the districts who have the skills and knowledge and do the work. The residents of the Capitol reflect the largely unproductive lifestyles of our own rich, born aloft by inherited wealth and illusory property bubbles.

Financialisation – the rapid growth of finance sectors to increasingly dominate the economy and politics – has characterized advanced capitalist countries since the 1980s. As Tony McKenna notes, this has encouraged a delusional mentality among elites that deteriorating growth and rates of profit can be off-set by what Marx referred to as fictitious capital. The Capitol is partying on borrowed money, as well as borrowed labor.

As Thomas Piketty demonstrated in his *Capital in the 21st Century*, there's been a growing imbalance between labor and capital due to the rise of inherited and asset wealth. A tiny plutocracy perches at the top, possessing awesome economic and political power. Below them is another part of the elite who also gain from capital, what Piketty calls patrimonial capitalism, that is, wealth gained through inheritance rather than entrepreneurship.

At the other end of the scale, as Guy Standing (*The Precariat*) has set out, there is a salariat, with some employment security, pensions, paid holidays and other non-wage perks. But they (the lower middle class, essentially) are shrinking, and the old proletariat is also dwindling, undermined by cuts to welfare, eroding secure and stable enmployment, and attacks on unions. What has grown is the precariat, who experience unstable labor, are subject to "flexible" contracts, and work mainly as temps, casuals and freelancers. This creates a continual consciousness of deprivation, of anxiety, anomie, alienation – and anger.

"All I can think of is the emaciated bodies of the children at our kitchen table"

Income inequality in the United States is at a 50-year high, and the rich pay less tax than the poor. If Panem seems exaggerated – why doesn't the Capitol just share out a bit more of "its" wealth? – we might ask the same question in our own world. The answer is that the Capitol doesn't care.

Research suggests that wealth is an empathy killer. The more sheltered we are, the fewer types of people we feel comfortable with or have any insight into the lives of (Daisy Grewal, "How Wealth Reduces Compassion", *Scientific American*, 10 April 2012). We're also more likely to believe disinformation about others.

But maybe this is the wrong question. Panem's economic system is subservient to its politics. The Capitol's segregation of the districts according to what they produce, its creation of artificial scarcity, its monopolization of resources, these are primarily political. They aren't the best way to structure an economy, but they are a good way to control a populace while appropriating their labor.

This is really what "neoliberalism" means, a way of preserving massive inequalities in wealth and power, from the local to the global level. And now especially in collapse.

"You won't be going to the Capitol"

When capitalized, the "Capitol" references to the United States Capitol, the building in Washington, DC that hosts Congress, the legislative branch of the federal government. The word comes from Latin and is associated with the Temple of Jupiter Optimus Maximus on Capitoline Hill, one of the seven hills of Rome. It signifies any center of political power and concentration of elite influence.

Like many real world capitals, Panem's is not just a center of power but also of wealth. Both "capital" and "capitol" are derived from the Latin root *caput*, meaning head. Capital evolved from the words *capitālis*, "of the head," and *capitāle*, "wealth." In *The Hunger Games*, this center is cruel and corrupt. The United States may be unusual in its capital not being its wealthiest conurbation, but its republic is still corrupted by a nexus of mutual interests that come together in its governing city.

Of course, the Roman Empire also exulted in its wealth and power, but decadence, corruption and overreach ensured it couldn't last forever.

"Here there would be no shortages. Ever"

Any story that depicts an oppressive state and an exploitative economy is likely to attract libertarian interpretations. Even some leftist commentators interpret the series this way. But if Suzanne Collins wanted to write a (right-wing) libertarian story it would be obvious. Such stories tend to be explicit in their politics, and most of them are terrible. Ayn Rand's novels are just one example. *The Hunger Games* is the anti-Rand.

The series doesn't critique a socialist state. There are no hypocritical appeals by the Capitol elite to equality, no rhetoric about a workers' state. Instead, there are conservative appeals to statist nationalism, patriotism and punishment. Neither is there any Rand-style conquering hero, certain of his exceptionalism but held back by equality; our hero is modest and self-doubting, trapped in a world of extreme differences.

There's no nominal system of representation through which the ruling party claims it receives the will of the people. There's just President Snow and his subservients, an outright oligarchy. The design of the Capitol is also effete rather than Soviet brutalist in style, an extension of elite architecture from our time, combined with aspects of Roman-style grandeur as adored by twentieth-century fascists.

Panem is modeled on the present United States, which was hardly heading toward socialism when Collins began developing her world. Rather, the concern was about a right-wing regime, the George W. Bush administration, that had exploited a terrible event to promote war and marginalize dissent, introduce sweeping surveillance and distract from corporate power. Collins is clearly most concerned with conflict, environmental destruction and economic exploitation. How often do libertarian stories give a damn about those things?

"One more time? For the audience?"

The Hunger Games is about where right-wing "libertarianism" is taking us, not that far in the future.

At first sight, Panem looks like a state-controlled economy. But there are privately-owned businesses, including small business owners and merchants. Indeed, this is an aspect of class difference in the districts. Even in District 12, there's a market and shops that serve the wealthier townspeople. The Capitol doesn't care if there's a small business owning class, indeed it suits its strategy of divide and rule. What's more important is that it receives the vast majority of the wealth that the workers of Panem produce.

It's not a socialist command economy; there are no apparent attempts to rationalize production according to scientific principles. It's capitalism run amok: corrupt, oligarchical, decadent and necessarily authoritarian, with no workers' rights, environmental protection, welfare or healthcare for the poor, social responsibility to burden the elite, or democracy to restrain their rule.

What right-wing libertarians see in Panem as a critique of leftist statism – an economy that restricts people's freedom and provides little opportunity for advancement, is heavily policed and concentrates wealth and power in the hands of a few – is exactly what they should be critical of today and yet happily justify as long as it's called "capitalism."

Most importantly, as we'll see, the story promotes a very different set of values to right-wing libertarianism. Cooperation and collaboration are crucial to surviving the Capitol's Games.

"I have to admit I didn't see it coming"

Panem's 1 percent exist in our world. But it's not just rich people running government, it's the increasing fusion of state and corporations. Benito Mussolini, the founder of modern fascism, declared that "Fascism should more properly be called corporatism because it is the merger of state and corporate power." He suggested it meant we should be, "Barely able to slip a cigarette paper between corporations and government." We're getting there. The rich, especially the super-rich and corporate owners, get much richer. They buy, literally, political influence, or just take up government positions and introduce policies to make themselves even richer. Which then allows them to buy more political influence, and so on. It makes sense that it's billionaires who are funding the new authoritarians all around the world.

This has also enabled the increasing monopolization of the economy. Forty years of the neoliberal experiment, which it was claimed would create a much more dynamic and diverse economy, has done the opposite. It doesn't really matter if there are still some small business owners, since they can't hope to challenge the Amazons, Walmarts, Googles and Apples of our Capitol economy. Indeed, Amazon is the perfect corporation for this fictional world: a company that generates enormous wealth for its founder and exercises autocratic control over its many impoverished, surveilled workers. A Panemian state in itself, a corporate Capitol.

"I guess the odds aren't exactly in my favor"

Some commentators suggest that *The Hunger Games* doesn't critique capitalism because it depicts a cyber-feudal society that depends on direct expropriation from the districts rather than manipulative market mechanisms. But at this point, what's the difference? The ordinary people of Panem don't own their labor or its products, indeed they're "fetishized" for them, organized according to what they do. And still they starve.

The districts are responsible for all of the country's output but they must "export" almost all of it to serve the Capitol's insatiable appetite. As a result, many districts such as 11 and 12 don't even have enough coal to power their own districts or enough food to feed their residents, despite producing these goods themselves.

Specialization also means that the districts, like regions such as Appalachia, remain dependent. As noted, extractive industries owned by outsiders create a legacy of poverty. The simplicity of some of the districts' products doesn't allow related industries to develop. It's probably not a coincidence that some of the other districts which produce more complicated products are also more privileged by the Capitol.

As Joel Kotkin argues in *The Coming of Neo-Feudalism*, America is reverting to a feudal age. Income growth has skewed dramatically toward the ultra-rich, creating a ruling financial and now tech oligarchy. As Kotkin suggests, this generational shift will shape our future economic, political and social order.

Just like a feudal order, there are "laws" to the market, forces that can't be challenged, for example, poverty wages for many workers in certain industries, or massive pay rises and bonuses for CEOs. But who gets what is actually determined by power. The Capitol rigs the economy of Panem to divide workers and keep them weak. There's nothing natural about it.

"It's to the Capitol's advantage to have us divided among ourselves"

Elites fear nothing so much as the districts uniting to challenge them. Most obviously, there's the segregation of the workers in their slave factory areas, policed by force. We could be talking about Panem, or Chinese megafactory complexes churning out smartphones and laptops, or unsafe warehouses in Bangladesh where women and children sweat to produce disposable fast fashion for shopping mall chains.

Then there are other forms of division and class management. Energy, food and other resources are doled out according to whether the districts please the Capitol. Again, it's political. Districts 1, 2 and 4 have a better relationship with the Capitol and receive more. It's calculated by class management, by what best protects the Capitol and serves its greed.

This also happens within the districts, for example the difference between the dirty, dangerous work done by the poor families of the Seam, compared to the relatively privileged family businesses (for example Peeta's family bakery). This resembles the US class system in which the wealthy preserve their control by pitting the middle class against the poor.

Suzanne Collins might not be a Marxist. But in her series she depicts a deeply divisive exploitative economy based on our own. It's why Andrew Slack, founder of fan activism organization The Harry Potter Alliance, calls *The Hunger Games* "arguably the most anti-classist blockbuster in history."

"I've never been a contender in these Games anyway"

In the film adaptation of the first book, President Snow explains to Seneca the Gamemaker the reason for the Hunger Games. He could easily pick 24 children from the districts and shoot them, but the important thing is to have a winner. This gives people a glimmer of hope: "A little hope is fine. A lot of hope is dangerous. A spark is fine, as long as it's contained."

Collins suggests how the system manages dissent through a modicum of meritocracy. The economy offers no possibility of advancement, but through the Games there's the promise to the victors of a life of luxury and the adulation of the Capitol (though never to become an actual Capitolist). Of course, it's a small chance, first to be chosen for and then to survive the tournament. While the Games strike terror in the poorer districts, competing in them is something that some young people in the career districts actually hunger for.

It's frequently forgotten that the term "meritocracy" was not meant to be taken literally. It was coined in 1958 by the sociologist Michael Young in his essay *The Rise of the Meritocracy* as a satire of the seemingly merit-based education system in the UK at the time. Young claimed that this system only appeared to reward the intelligent and hard-working; in reality its testing masked a selection process that served the already privileged, rather like the pre-Games judges' scoring system in *The Hunger Games* that favors the career tributes who have been training from a young age.

The politics of Young's satire can be surmised from the origins of his newly-created word, a combination of the Latin root for "earn" and the Ancient Greek for "power" or "rule." He was pointing to how a seemingly fair approach covers for a class system. Even if a few can climb into privilege, this doesn't justify the wealth of the Capitol. In a deeply unjust system, meritocracy is a myth. The odds are never in our favor.

"And who hasn't broken the law?"

In Panem, fascist terror is used to crush dissent. The Capitol promises that its domination is the only chance we have for peace, all the while it maintains itself through violence.

In poorer countries, those that supply so many of our goods in Western countries, workers really are policed and punished. But in the richer West as well, our societies are increasingly managed and policed, in aggressive racially and socially biased policing, immigration raids, detention camps for refugees including children, bailiffs and bail "officers"...

Then there's the criminal justice system, which also performs a class function. The US has the highest prison population and highest percentage of prisoners per capita in the world, higher than in the former Soviet Union under Stalin. Half of all inmates are imprisoned for drug offenses, 80 percent for possession. There are 5 million more people under supervision. And millennials are the most incarcerated generation in history; more than half of the people in state prisons are aged 20-30.

A fair society wouldn't need to lock up so many of its own people. It's a way to manage poverty and inequality. It produces substantial profits for private prison owners, including enforced prison labor, not really so different from Panem's slave factory economy.

It's also deeply racist. As Michelle Alexander argues in *The New Jim Crow*, by targeting particularly black men through the War on Drugs and decimating communities of color, the American criminal justice system functions as a system of racial control relegating millions to a permanent second-class status.

Even after people are released, they're treated as a stigmatized caste and disenfranchised, ill-equipped for survival in an economy that if you're poor doesn't allow for mistakes (it's different if you're wealthy). It's not suprising: the criminal justice system reflects the same values of violence, hatred, shame, greed, classism and racism as the society they're part of. Freedom for some, fences for many.

"I'm done killing their slaves for them"

An underclass, already forced to pay tribute to a state that neglects it, presses its youth into violent service to benefit the wealthy and powerful.

Since the Capitol's residents are not known for fighting, the majority of Panem's military police come from District 2. The Capitolists who are in the military are commanders (however, there's a reference to many of the Capitol's residents being so in debt that they're forced to join the Peacekeepers, where their debts are forgiven).

After the first rebellion in which the Capitol lost its main military district in District 13, a new base was established in District 2. Money and work poured into the district. This was how Peacekeeper became a common position for residents from the district, and why it looks more favorably on the Capitol than many of the other districts.

Militarism is a key theme for Suzanne Collins. Her father, a military specialist, historian and doctor of political science, was a great influence on the story. He served in Vietnam and apparently suffered nightmares after his return. Collins has said that her father made sure his children understood why wars occurred, how they played out and their consequences.

The books were written in the shadow of the Iraq and Afghanistan wars and the so-called War on Terror, in which young people were sacrificed and many more were wounded and traumatized, another major theme in the series. The average age of soldiers in these wars has been 19 years old. A total of 90 percent of all casualties have been younger than 21.

Militarism and "defence" spending is used particularly in poor areas to buy support, and joining the armed forces provides employment where otherwise there is little. In *The Hunger Games*, the reaping represents a kind of compulsory draft, but in our world, economic compulsion does the job. The tesserae particularly entice the poorest into "service." The children of the Capitol experience no such pressures.

Militarism also propagandizes violence and domination. The Games themselves are a patriotic national spectacle. The players are paraded in front of cheering crowds and politicians make grand speeches. The Capitol audience appears to adore the young people, who are costumed and trained before being sent to their deaths. Those who die have their pictures broadcast at the end of each day, just like the nightly news when troops are killed in combat. The hypocrisy is obvious.

"It's mostly a lot of blather about what we owe the Capitol"

Militarism is related to imperialism, another major part of the series. Witness the Capitol's grand neoclassical architecture, how major characters from the Capitol share the names of ancient Romans, the use of chariots to introduce the tributes to the audience, and of course the gladiatorial Games.

Imperialism is embedded in the economic structure of Panem. Empires, whether formal military expanses or international economic regimes, require regions to seize and control. There's always an extraction zone from which materials are taken without full payment, and a disposal zone, where costs are dumped in the form of dangerous jobs, waste and pollution.

The idea that *The Hunger Games* isn't anti-capitalist because it depicts a brutal dictatorship rather than a more recognizably capitalist "liberal democracy" comes from a privileged first world viewpoint. From a global perspective, capitalism is brutal and exploitative, frequently extractive and heavily policed.

Collins' description of outlying districts providing mostly raw materials to a conquering central power parallels what sociologists call World-systems theory, the best known version of which was developed by Immanuel Wallerstein. This sees the world as a single order rather than separate nation states. The transnational division of labor (who produces what) consists of core, semi-periphery and periphery countries. Core countries focus on higher skill, capital-intensive production, while the rest of the world focuses on low-skill, labor-intensive production and the extraction of raw materials.

Core nations are able to purchase raw materials and other goods from non-core nations at low prices and exploit their cheap labor, but demand higher prices for their exports back to the non-core – a kind of trade tribute to be paid by poorer countries (one that, historically, the colonized were forced to celebrate by acknowledging the "naturalness" of colonial domination).

This reinforces the core's dominance and keeps the periphery underdeveloped.

In recent decades, more skilled jobs have been outsourced from rich to poorer nations. But from the perspective of large corporations this not only increases profits, it also depresses wages back home and erodes workers' rights. The game is rigged by and for the Capitol.

"They certainly don't have a problem watching children being murdered every year"

What's so insidious about this is that not only do core Capitol countries keep some countries poor today, in many ways they made them poor in the first place. As Daron Acemoglu and James Robinson note in *Why Nations Fail* (originally described in a paper with Simon Johnson), 500 years ago some European countries were poorer than prosperous areas of Latin America. When Spanish conquistadors arrived, they stole the gold, put native populations to work, and set up extractive institutions to drain as many resources (silver, gold, food) as possible from the land while keeping power in the hands of a small elite.

As Acemoglu and Robinson suggest, once extractive institutions are established they're hard to get rid of. For example, in Africa, many of whose modern states were created by European colonialists, these injustices led eventually to mass resistance and the overthrow of colonial rule. But in almost every case, the new elite simply seized the same extractive institutions for themselves.

Western capitols didn't become rich and powerful due to natural talent or historical inevitability. They dominated the districts of the global South to become rich and powerful.

"But you have to admit, the food's prime"

An example: the past 50 years have seen the consolidation of a global food regime based on exports from poorer countries of so-called "cash crops." This regime has encouraged countries to focus on a small number of agricultural products, or sometimes non-food commodities which take up prime agricultural land. Loans and repayment demands are used by Western capitols to reinforce the system.

The more the districts serve the Capitol, the more vulnerable they are. Most of the countries that experienced rising undernourishment during the 2010s are highly dependent on commodity exports and/or imports. Many high commodity-dependent countries have rising hunger or a worsening food crisis.

This process of specialization has displaced peasant farmers (including by force), strengthened Western agri-food oligopolies and transformed many countries from food self-sufficiency into food deficit. Hunger and malnutrition result from increasingly monopolized markets, poverty and inequality, and corruption. We've created incredible abundance for some, punishing scarcity for many others. Western and corrupt influences try to blame the victims, that the "solution" must be for local farmers to increase their productivity, when the real problem has been neglect of smallholder agriculture in favor of predatory global corporations. But, of course, the Capitol only cares about its own appetites.

"How despicable we must seem to you"

The Hunger Games is often described as a dystopia, a fictional warning about the future. But it's more of a critical description of our past and present. In fact, the word "dystopia" derives from colonial history. In 1868, the British philosopher economist John Stuart Mill was the first to use it as its own word: "It is, perhaps, too complimentary to call them Utopians," Mill stated in a Parliamentary speech criticizing Britain's colonial rule in Ireland. "They ought rather to be called dys-topians...what they appear to favor is too bad to be practicable."

If this was just history, it would be bad enough. And historically, capitalism was brutal and exploitative, with dangerous working conditions and factories, punishingly long working hours, and child labor. But it's not history; for so many people it's the present.

Slavery still exists in our world. Today's slave labor mostly involves poor people in developing countries being exploited in clothing and shoe factories. Across the world, 25 million people are victims of forced labor. Most of them are exploited by companies for profit, rather than by private individuals.

But using the analogy of *The Hunger Games*, many of us live in both the Capitol and the districts. Given increasing inequality and decreasing opportunity, we're highly unlikely to join the real Capitol elite. At the same time, if we're lucky enough to experience even a modicum of comfort and security, we're also like the crowds in the Capitol, looking away as the districts slave to supply us with goods, and uninterested in the dangerous, dirty conditions in which they live from which we benefit.

"Nothing says perfection like white"

The Capitol is also a structure of white supremacy. This is suggested first of all by the whiteness of President Snow: white hair, clothes, roses, his sense of Southern US "gentility." It's easy to imagine him as a plantation owner, which he is really.

While there appear to be a range of ethnicities among the residents of the Capitol, there's a much greater diversity in the districts. The residents of District 11, the agricultural and second poorest district located in the southeast, are mainly black. They live in small shacks and dress like they're in the Antebellum South. An electrified fence surrounds them, 30 feet high and topped with razor wire, with guard towers evenly spaced along it.

Since the residents of the Capitol are a mixture of ethnicities, our focus is meant to be on Panem's economic structure, how it creates and exploits division and keeps people separated. As Ibram X. Kendi (*How to Be an Antiracist*) argues, racism is an economic structure. We tend to focus on racist attitudes and suggest they create the system, but it's the other way around. Racist ideas and attitudes are constructed and promoted to serve racist systems.

The most obvious example is slavery in the United States, a system of economic exploitation that benefited an elite, justified by viewing black people as subhuman. It was an advanced surveillance state, the high-tech Capitol of its day. As examined by the *New York Times'* 1619 project, this system shaped American capitalism in ways we experience today: the commoditization of people, scientific accounting and measurement, the combination of incentives and punishments, oppressive and intrusive management techniques, all designed to constantly increase workers' productivity.

It's also had a broader political legacy, to divide and rule those who have common interests. Slavery provided white workers with what W. E. B. Du Bois called a "public and psychological wage," a sense of freedom and entitlement compared to slaves, even as it pulled down all workers' wages – poverty and hunger helping to contain all but the elite.

"It's the finale"

Liberals seem to be continually surprised by contemporary events – by the behavior of the new authoritarian populist leaders, abuses of corporate power and the waning appeal of their own politics. They fail to realize we've entered into an era in which a new form of totalitarianism has emerged.

Sheldon Wolin's *Democracy Incorporated* was published in the same year as the first *Hunger Games* book. If the latter dramatizes where we're headed, the former is an important analysis of a new totalitarianism that's already emerged, and there are parallels between the two.

Inverted totalitarianism differs in important ways from previous totalitarianisms. For example, it's anti-collectivist and idealizes individualism and adulates celebrities. We also think of fascism as being about the state, but as Wolin suggests, "Inverted totalitarianism is only in part a state-centered phenomenon. Primarily it represents the political coming of age of corporate power and the political demobilization of the citizenry." In this new totalitarianism, corporate power is incorporated into the very structure of the state: "Superpower is the union of state and corporation in an age of waning democracy and political illiteracy...[C]orporate power and its culture are no longer external forces that occasionally influence politics and legislation. As these have become integral, so the citizenry has become marginal and democracy more manageable."

But just like previous fascisms, inverted totalitarianism proclaims its nationalism and patriotism, including support for the military. Since globalizing multinational capitalism has no national loyalty, these play an important role in providing people with a common identity and sense of belonging. Most of them may not have any real enthusiasm for fascism, but nationalism and patriotism make them less likely to make democratic demands and more accepting of fear and power.

In their own ways, both *Democracy Incorporated* and *The Hunger Games* help to describe what we're seeing: the fusion of corporate and state power, showbusiness and spectacle in place of democratic deliberation and participation, the celebration of the nation and national identity. The new Panem – in our world.

"I don't think I really understood the Capitol until now"

Collins is saying something radical for a mainstream cultural phenomenon: the United States is becoming a new kind of neo-fascist state.

Any society that allows itself to become radically unequal

eventually ends in an uprising or a police state, or one followed by the other. Now we need to add collapse to our understanding of what's new in the new authoritarian politics. Whether we read *The Hunger Games* in generational, geographical, historical, colonial, economic, environmental or class terms, it depicts our most likely endgame.

Propaganda about freedom and free markets will be replaced by calls for security for a few and serfdom for many. The Capitol will openly serve corporate interests against workers. Control will be achieved through state repression and economic segregation, an authoritarian capitalism. These regimes will favor older people and contain and immiserate the young. The serfs will be heavily policed and militarized, aided by advanced technology and near-total surveillance, a digitized dictatorship. Media spectacle and shock tactics – perhaps some future version of the Hunger Games, probably a punishment for "political dissidents" – will be used to deter popular resistance.

For the masses, the system will induce exhaustion and a focus on survival. A minimal meritocracy will buy-off a small part of the non-elite, but in reality social advancement will be very limited. This new order will not be popular, but it will be justified as necessary to preserve society against "hostile forces."

This system needs a name. Call it capitolism.

Chapter 5

"Happy Hunger Games!"

"Ten, nine, eight, seven, six, five, four, three, two, one..."

The Hunger Games are a televised gladiatorial combat event in which 24 teenagers, called tributes, are forced to fight to the death in a deadly, natural-looking but actually artificial arena. The winning tribute and their home district are rewarded with food and riches. The Games provide entertainment for the Capitol. Most importantly, they remind the districts of its overwhelming power.

Panem's rulers present the Games as a celebration, and also perversely an unending punishment for the districts' past rebellion. But the Games embody the Capitol's ideology in a deeper way. They try to normalize a destructive set of social "values" which serve the elite, namely brutal competitive individualism among the poor. This is really why the Games are so important to the Capitol.

But this also means we can use the Games to reveal what's so twisted about the Capitol and its rule – and since *The Hunger Games* are a critical reflection of our world, what's so wrong with capitalism. That the Capitol invests so much in the Games is significant, that it has to try so hard to hijack what we would otherwise know to be true: the games they make us play are not natural at all.

"Ladies and gentlemen, let the 74th Hunger Games begin!"

The Hunger Games are a high-tech, carefully choreographed, basely brutal, heavily marketed mandatory mega-ritual. In what is for most people in Panem a harsh, grinding existence, the Games are meant to provide a brutal annual purging, some kind of relief through bloodletting, in which rage is directed inwards between the districts rather than upwards toward the elite. (We learn in the prequel *The Ballad of Songbirds and Snakes* that it took a while for the Gamemakers to perfect their recipe for the extravaganza; to begin with, many people in the Capitol didn't watch it.)

It's ironic that *The Hunger Games* has sometimes been critiqued as rebeltainment, one of the ways that the frustrated masses, especially young people, can imagine a revolution that will never come to pass. Ironic, because the point of the story is to critique exactly this. It's a story about how an authoritarian regime uses spectacle to allow its masses to let off some steam in order to avert a rebellion against its rule. It's meant to reveal how a regime manipulates people through media.

The Games are a fusion of TV-media-cruelty-politics, which couldn't be more contemporary. The spectacle and cruelty are just the means. The political aim of the Games is to promote power and induce hopelessness. *The Hunger Games* is not about reality TV as such, critiques of which are nothing new. It's about the propaganda purposes of media used in ways to try to shape our reality, and how they support the political and economic aims of a regime.

"Make sure you get it on camera"

Quite a few sci-fi dystopian stories have used the idea of a violent future sport as a means of pacifying and controlling society, such as *Rollerball*, *The Running Man*, *Punishment Park*, the short stories *The Lottery* and *The Most Dangerous Game*...Some are more political than others. But it's the broader politics and political economy of *The Hunger Games* that makes it stand out. Otherwise it would mainly be an action adventure story, which it's not. It's not *fun*.

Most often, *The Hunger Games* has been compared to *Battle*

Royale (*Batoru Rowaiaru*), a Japanese dystopian thriller film released in 2000, directed by Kinji Fukasaku and written by Kenta Fukasaku, and based on the 1999 novel by Koushun Takami. The story follows a group of junior high school students who are forced to fight to the death by a totalitarian Japanese state. Following a major recession, the government passes the BR (Battle Royale) Act to control the nation's youth. One class is chosen to participate in the annual event; they are provided with rations and have 3 days to fight until a victor emerges (explosive collars are fitted to kill any "uncooperative" students).

Suzanne Collins says she wasn't aware of *Battle Royale* before she published her first *Hunger Games* book. In any case, the theme of violent generational conflict didn't start with *Battle Royale*. William Golding's 1954 *Lord of the Flies* represents a Hobbesian war of all against all between stranded school children. In turn, this echoes Ödön von Horvath's 1937 *Jugend Ohne Gott* (*The Age of the Fish*, also known as *Youth without God*), in which a teacher has to supervise a gang of young Nazis at a summer camp in the mountains and where the starving locals are regarded as prey...

Some commentators see *Battle Royale* as a satire of the Japanese economy during its Lost Decade. Others view it as a criticism of the country's educational system, its fiercely competitive nationwide examinations and tough employment market (reflecting the pressures on young people noted in Chapter 2). Other interpretations include Japanese generational attitudes that have created social, political and economic divides between the generations. Meanwhile, the film's director stated that his wartime experience led him to realize that the Japanese government was lying about the Second World War, and he developed a burning hatred of adults that he maintained for a long time.

"This is the final word in entertainment"

More recently, "battle royale" has become the term for a genre of videogame in particular in which a group of people are dropped into an arena and fight to the death until there is one winner. Games in this genre include *PlayerUnknown's Battlegrounds, Fortnite Battle Royale, Day Z, H1Z1: King of the Kill, Apex Legends* and *Call of Duty: Black Ops 4*'s Blackout mode.

Battle royale makes for an almost perfect format, combining action and strategy and depending on skill and good luck. Each relatively brief game session builds to a tense climax. One characteristic of the genre is that the arena shrinks over time, heightening the action. After an initial period in which competitors hunt for supplies, they're forced to confront each other as the play area closes in.

There's a cultural resonance about this virtual war against all, often in a post-apocalyptic wasteland, involving a fight for meager supplies, and alliances between players which everyone knows cannot last. Mirroring survivalist culture, these worlds are inherently individualistic, violent and winner-takes-all.

The Hunger Games largely predates this genre, but its arenas echo videogames. At first sight they appear to be natural environments, but they're carefully designed levels sculpted by the Gamemakers, with traps, special events that can be triggered whenever the action flags, a range of "player characters" in the tributes, and loot boxes in the form of the sponsors' gifts. Movie adaptations of videogames have become notorious for being bad and for failing to capture the feel (or purpose) of the source material. And of course, often there's no purpose, no rationale provided, for why the players are fighting. Who designed the arenas, and how do they benefit from them?

Perhaps, despite the title of the series, *The Hunger Games* manages to draw on videogame conventions without sucking because the Games themselves aren't really the focus, and because, much like the residents of the districts, we come to fear the Games and hate what they force the main characters to do.

It's also interesting that there's been no proper videogame

adaptation of *The Hunger Games*, despite it seeming an obvious fit. There was a free promotional videogame that involved managing Katniss to achieve a series of tasks, but not fighting for survival in the arena. Even in the arena of violent video games, it's unacceptable to have digital kids killing digital kids.

"No viewer could turn away from the show now"

As Suzanne Collins has stated:

> Bread crops up a lot in *The Hunger Games*. It's the main food source in the districts, as it was for many people historically...But there's a dark side to bread, too. When [Head Gamemaker] Plutarch Heavensbee references it, he's talking about Panem et Circenses, Bread and Circuses, where food and entertainment lull people into relinquishing their political power. Bread can contribute to life or death in *The Hunger Games*.

"Bread and circuses" refers to the Roman Caesars' strategy of quelling public discontent by providing people with food and entertainment. (Of course, the Capitol doesn't really provide the bread; even the name of the country is a lie.) The phrase was coined by the Roman satirist Juvenal, describing how the state pacified its subjects by distracting them from political reality. The entertainment was largely provided by gladiatorial games. In *The Hunger Games*, Seneca the Gamemaker's name alludes to Lucius Annaeus Seneca, one of the men thought responsible for the games.

In the novels and films, these contests are crossed with reality television techniques to create Panem's Hunger Games. The setting draws a link between Ancient Rome and the present-day United States, with the almost limitless distractions provided by the latter's media entertainment complex taking the role of the gladiatorial games.

As noted, twentieth century fascists also used Roman design and iconography, emphasizing power and empire, and the grand introduction of the tributes has something of the staging of the Nazi Olympics. Again, Collins is suggesting the US is proto-fascist, or soon could be.

"It's the first gift that's always the hardest to pay back"

In addition, Collins was inspired by the myth of Theseus and the Minotaur. "The myth tells how in punishment for past deeds, Athens periodically had to send seven youths and seven maidens to Crete, where they were thrown into the Labyrinth and devoured by the monstrous Minotaur." Again, this was a projection of political and economic power, with Crete acting as a supposed custodian of peace and trade – another aspect of the Hobbesian "promise" that, without order imposed from above, people won't be able to procure the means of daily survival through their own commerce and cooperation.

This Hobbesian state of nature propaganda enables the state to in effect extract a tribute from us. "Tribute" is cleverly chosen by Collins, since it has two meanings: something given or contributed voluntarily as due or deserved, a gift or service showing respect or affection; or alternatively, a payment by one ruler or nation to another in acknowledgment of submission and subjugation or as the price of protection, imposed by a government, sovereign or landlord, having the power of coercion. To the latter meaning, it often also has a criminal connotation as well, such as protection money to the mob. The last implication is the most radical. The oligarchic state is akin to a criminal enterprise, which uses the threat of violence to subjugate and extract wealth from the people.

"No one watches and they don't have a game"

We noted Suzanne Collins' inspiration for the series in Chapter

2. She identified several problems with reality television, "the voyeuristic thrill – watching people being humiliated, or brought to tears or suffering physically...There's also the potential for desensitizing the audience, so that when they see real tragedy playing out on, say, the news, it doesn't have the impact it should."

The titles alone of well-known programs indicate the "values" they promote: *Big Brother, Survivor, American Gladiators, Fear Factor, Naked and Afraid*...Critics have suggested how reality TV combines neoliberal ideology (competition, individualism, the offer of instant wealth, the humiliating "elimination" of losers) with the normalization of a surveillance society (discussed later).

Although reality TV provides a frame for part of the series, it's not really its political focus. But Collins clearly wants to re-sensitize modern audiences to the perversity of this kind of programming by taking its stakes a significant step further. Neither the books or the films are particularly graphic, but they are unflinching. As *The Guardian* put it: "The vicious use of Warhol's 15 minutes to oppress and cheapen the public is not presented with distancing black comedy, more a protracted growl of pain."

Current reality TV trades in humilation and suffering, even if not yet in the murder of participants (there have however been cases of participants committing suicide as a result of appearing on these exploitative shows). But as Collins suggests, the point isn't so much that enjoying the pain of TV show contestants is a sickness in itself, it's how the erosion of our sense of decency has wider social consequences. We become numb to the hunger games, conflict and exploitation in the real world.

Katniss of course represents this numbing response. While she feels a connection with her hunting partner Gale, she's quick to deny any emotion ("...the way the girls stare at him...It makes me jealous but not for the reason people think. Good hunting partners are hard to find"). At this point she hasn't experienced the trauma of the Games; it's her environment that's numbed her – the cruelty, exploitation and violence built into the state and the poverty it uses to crush people.

We live in a reality TV culture, of celebrity gossip and scandal of course, but most importantly, increasingly of politics as infotainment, which just like the spectacle of reality TV helps us to forget that real people's lives are affected by the games they play in the Capitol. Prompted by the fictional Panem, seeing how the Capitol constructs the Games and feeling empathy with the young people dragged into its brutality, we're reminded to consider the ways that similar techniques are used to distance us from what's really happening: the TV adverts aimed at young people to join the military, the militainment that glorifies force and lethal technology in movies and videogames, the marginalization and demonization of migrants and refugees as a dangerous invasion of subhumans...

As Roger Ebert put it in his review of the first *Hunger Games* film: "A vision of present-day America is summoned up, its citizenry glutted with fast food and distracted by reality TV. How is the population expected to accept the violent sacrifice of 24 young lives a year? How many have died in our recent wars?"

But the values we associate with military service and atomized accomplishment don't derive from our own natures, they're continually promoted as a means of control, just as Panem's dictators want the districts to give up their children and be happy about it.

"Hijacked"

In other respects, we're becoming increasingly sensitized.

Demagogues love politics to be conducted at the level of rhetorical, and then real, violence. This creates and contributes to the Hobbesian world they need in order to keep us scared and compliant.

We can be hijacked by their rhetorical violence, literally in biological terms. When we feel threatened, a fight-or-flight response can kick in, overwhelming our capacity for reason, a phenomenon some psychologists call amygdala hijack (for example, Daniel Goleman in his 1995 book *Emotional Intelligence*).

The amygdala is a collection of cells near the base of the brain. There are two, one in each hemisphere. This is where feelings are remembered, and attached to associations and responses – our emotional coding. When the threat is mild or moderate, the frontal lobes overrule the amygdala, and we typically respond in rational, appropriate ways. However, when the threat is strong (or perceived as such), the amygdala can overpower the frontal lobes, triggering the fight-or-flight response which can produce sudden, illogical and irrational overreactions, often strong anger, aggression or fear.

This response was appropriate for early humans because of more prevalent threats of physical harm. Today, there may be far fewer physical threats, at least for many of us, but we experience psychological threats from the pressures and stresses of modern life. Demagogues can exploit these phsyiological responses, particularly by creating and emphasizing otherness, insecurity and scarcity.

In Suzanne Collins' series, the Capitol, in addition to its propaganda and the Hunger Games, has a direct mechanism to induce fear in genetically modified creatures known as tracker jackers. These swarming wasp-like insects have a venom which, as Katniss puts it, is "carefully created to target the place where fear lives in your brain." These creatures stem from the first rebellion, when they were placed by the Capitol around the districts like landmines.

Despite day-to-day life being much safer than it was for many people, we're still surrounded by psychological landmines. Take social media platforms, which make money through the algorithmic amplification of sensational, deliberately triggering, harmful content, often micro targeted at us – the perfect vehicles for the misinformation and manipulation that demagogues need to seize power.

Katniss is scared, of course, but in a way her resignation about her chances helps her to manage it. Her focus becomes how she'll die, whether it can be with some dignity, and maybe even a little dissent as well...

"This awful piece of time we call today"

In *The Hunger Games,* as an audience we're spectators, but also spectators of spectators. We watch how different audiences react to the Games, particularly the contrast between the crowds in the Capitol who appear cheerfully compliant, and the residents of the districts who cower in fear.

For both audiences, in different ways, the Games breed political docility and submission. Beyond just advocating personal resistance to political repression, Suzanne Collins suggests the story illustrates how violence breeds docility: "I don't mean that threatening people with violence makes them docile, because it doesn't. I mean that teaching people to be violent and consume violence makes them docile." And further:

> The Games institutionalize a political docility not so much because they threaten violence to the districts' children, but because they create a society in which people think they must choose survival over solidarity. I think a lot of people, regardless of their political affiliation, feel like there has been a lot of being forced to choose survival over solidarity going around in the US.

(We'll return to solidarity in the next chapter.)

The books and films seem even more prescient today. Politics has become about TV moments of conflict and cruelty, like reality TV, with a violent emphasis, like a wrestling match. A reality TV president continually supplies new outrageous "plotlines" and controversies as a cover for corporate takeover and control and unchanging elite power. We risk becoming pacified toward children held in cages by government agents, cops gunning down suspects, refugees drowning, war atrocities, school shootings, white supremacists streaming mass murder… and politicians who do nothing but look on.

The effect is often to overwhelm us, turn many of us into spectators, whether out of a sense of distance, anxiety or resignation. It all seems too much, and the possibility of achieving collective change seems to recede from view.

"From the Gamemakers' point of view, this is the final word in entertainment"

If there are grounds for hope, one might be that, as *The Hunger Games* suggests, the masses are less suspectible to the Capitol's propaganda than it presumes. The Capitol presents the Games as a national pageant, but we see from the beginning that, in District 12 at least, the Games are endured, not enjoyed (the career districts may be a little different).

Perhaps the Capitol underestimates the districts. If the view from the Capitol is that the residents of the districts are just underclass scum, it makes sense that it's assumed they'd relish the violent spectacle of the Games. It's different though when you're also the target of the violence. So in Panem at least, the Games don't perform the typical role we assume of propaganda: distracting the masses from the reality of their lives, from exploitation and class division.

It's also significant that the Games are depicted as having most impact on the audience in the Capitol. The people of the districts are so lacking in hope (the Capitol assumes), that if they do hate the Games and despise its creators, it doesn't really matter. Rather, it's the more privileged districts and the Capitol itself that have to be made to celebrate in the Games, and by association, the Capitol's justification for exploiting its subjects.

It's this latter audience that most requires distraction. We know the Capitol audiences are so captured by consumerism and novelty that they constantly crave new entertainments, so the fresh "cast" of characters of each new Games, like the premiere of a favorite reality TV show, is an exciting annual event. The Gamemakers also have to ensure viewers don't become bored; they try to "direct" the Games and introduce new hazards if the action appears to be slowing and there haven't been any recent deaths.

The sentimental storyline of the "star-crossed lovers," as Katniss and Peeta are characterized, which the Gamemakers have to scramble to manage, also seems to be mostly for the audience in the Capitol. It's doutbful that the districts would believe that anyone fighting for their life in the arena would really have time for romance (as confirmed at the start of the second book, *Catching Fire,* when President Snow pays a menacing visit to Katniss and admits that: "Unfortunately, not everyone in the districts fell for your act"). To be that stupid, you'd have to live in the insulated comfort of the Capitol, a credulousness that Katniss and Peeta exploit in their struggle for survival (the irony of course is that Peeta genuinely does care for Katniss).

Mark Fisher ("Remember Who the Enemy Is", 25 November 2013, *k-punk*) makes this point:

> Part of what makes the novels and the films so powerful is the way they move beyond the consentimental affective regime imposed by reality TV, lachrymose advertising and soap operas. The greatness of Jennifer Lawrence's performances as Katniss consist in part in her capacity to touch on feelings – rage, horror, grim resolve – that have a political, rather than a privatised, register.

What all this echoes is that in our world, despite the elite's view of the stupidity of ordinary people, propaganda is often actually aimed most at elite audiences. After all, they have the most power and influence, and even if they're not part of the political leadership, they're critical to its legitimacy (as we'll note in Chapter 8, we later realize that the Capitol has already lost the support of some of its key figures, who have been waiting for the right moment to launch a revolution against its rule).

This reflects a point made in Edward S. Herman and Noam Chomsky's propaganda model (first presented in their *Manufacturing Consent: The Political Economy of the Mass Media*). It's not primarily poorer people who are hooked on political infotainment or insider political "controversies." Western democracies often rely on poorer people feeling so disenfranchised (sometimes literally) that they don't vote or engage in politics, so they don't really matter much for propaganda purposes. Most media coverage of politics focuses on issues with a bias toward richer audiences (who are also more valuable to advertisers), and cite elite sources for their authority. And so it is these audiences who are actually subject to the greatest amount of propaganda. They are the most complicit in the system, since they gain more from it than the poorest. If we're part of this social group, it's us, not the less privileged, who are the real dupes of the Capitol.

"I don't want them to change me in there. Turn me into some kind of monster that I'm not"

The Games aren't just a distraction. They also perform a propaganda role in establishing a dominant set of social values, values that legitimize the state's brutality and enforced inequality, and corrode the natural social solidarity that might threaten the Capitol. The Games model and promote, attempt to naturalize, the Capitol's broader ideology: brutal competitive individualism for the masses, eternal punishment for the poor, and a hopelessness that they can ever really win. They are the engineered embodiment of the degredation for which the Party in Orwell's *Nineteen Eighty-Four* strives: "In our world there will be no emotions except fear, rage, triumph, and self-abasement… Always, at every moment, there will be the thrill of victory, the sensation of trampling on an enemy who is helpless."

Even the Capitol's presentation of the Games – two young tributes from each district "to be trained in the art of survival and to be prepared to fight to the death" – is deceptive. The environment of the arena provides the illusion of choice: competitors can adopt different strategies and use whatever skills they like. They could even make the "choice" not to kill. But as noted, its meritocracy is a myth, since the career tributes typically win, and sponsors typically favor those most likely to prevail. It's possible to grant the Capitol credit that this may also be a conscious part of its ideological design for the Games, a way to reinforce that the game is rigged against the poorest districts from the start.

But in theory at least, the Games are every man and woman (child, really) for themselves (the supposedly natural elite of the Capitol never puts up its own competitors). The objective is to crush feelings of solidarity and interdependence between the districts, which is to say, the ordinary working and middle class (such as they are) of Panem. Much as how modern states use class, religious, ethnic and other differences to divide the working class and hinder their organization, Panem uses the Games to foster competition rather than cooperation between the districts, despite the fact that they have more in common with each other than anyone inside the Capitol's citadel. They literally get the districts to fight against each other.

"Maybe the other tributes are out there beating one another senseless. Which would be fine"

In *Catching Fire*, the second part of the story, Katniss remarks that, "Nobody decent ever wins the Games." Haymitch replies, "Nobody ever wins the Games. Period. There are survivors. There's no winners."

At first sight Panem may not resemble a "free market," but as we've discussed, there are more similarities between the two than we might think. The Games particularly model capitalist competition. We're compelled to see others as tributes. There are limited resources – artificially limited, in turns out, to force us to fight each other.

The only times that more supplies are made available, this too is designed to make competitors act more ruthlessly ("Feasts always result in fatalities"). This happens at the start of the Games to ensure an initial spectacular bloodbath, and later on, when the Gamemakers construct a "cornucopia" in the center of the arena, a treasury of weapons and supplies that the tributes can try to seize. Smartly, Katniss goes in the opposite direction, and later she destroys the cornucopia to try to level the playing field. It's a victory, but it still means she's trapped within the competitive logic of the Games, leaving the other tributes hungrier and more defenseless.

Survival and success in markets are unquestionable; there is no alternative to the arena, no space for solidarity and cooperation inside or outside it ("no emotions except fear, rage, triumph, and self-abasement"). The economic arena is a total capitolism: all pervasive, suffocating. Like the arena, there is no exit, except at the very end. We're instructed that the rules are unchangeable, even though the Gamemakers manipulate them for the Capitol's benefit. As competitors, we're fundamentally on our own. And we're told that the winners – in theory the strongest and smartest, but actually those most suited to this particular game – deserve all of the spoils.

In, for her, an unusual condemnatory moment, Katniss thinks of the career tributes: "Do you have any idea how much I hate you, I think. You, who have given your talents to the Games." But even if we hate the game (and the Capitol doesn't really care, as along as its capitolist realism seems inescapable), even if we see how the game is constructed, we find ourselves thinking that any alternative values such as kindness, compassion, collaboration are for losers. Like Katniss, we come to believe that such impulses, rather than being the only route to our collective survival, represent our greatest danger. This is the struggle then, for us to avoid becoming the monsters they most want us to be.

"Some walks you have to take alone"

A key mechanism in this, promoted by the Games, is distrust of others, which corrodes chances of cooperation, let alone solidarity.

Even before the brutal competition begins, we see how the Games and the need to act for the cameras to stand any chance of survival, sow doubt. When Katniss and Peeta are boarding the train for the Capitol, she wonders whether his apparent fear (he appears to have been crying) is an act, to trick the other tributes into thinking that he represents little threat in the Games.

This uncertainty about actions and motives runs through the Games, and indeed the whole story. Katniss is not by nature a cynical person, though she's understandably wary and closed off. But she's often unable to believe the truth of emotions displayed in front of her (much later in the story, however, her distrust of the motives of political actors will prove warranted).

Inside the Games, inside the system, as competitors we can't afford to see each other as people, instead we're tempted to turn others into commodities as well, evaluting people as threats, a combination of strengths and weaknesses according to the rules of the game.

This distrust makes sense. If we have to perform under capitalism – pretend to love our work, respect our boss, play psychological games with colleagues, act as if we like people even though we see them as competitors – we'll inevitably doubt others' actions as well.

"Nobody ever wins the Games"

The Games are only once a year, but they also reinforce the Hobbesian point that, however nasty and brutal they are, it's better to contain our supposedly "natural" violent and anti-social tendencies in the arena than for these forces to be unleashed. Proponents of capitalism make the same point: the market channels our "inherent" greed and competitiveness in "safe" ways, deliberately ignoring how it encourages them instead. Politics – democracy, collective deliberation, changing the game so that we can live by other values – are characterized by conservatives as "divisive," the route to all-out social conflict.

But if we can't find ways to resist it, the arena turns us into monsters anyway. This is underlined toward the end of the 74th Hunger Games in the attack of the mutts (muttations), recreations of tributes who have died earlier in the arena. It's the ultimate dehumanization of the tributes, meant to induce fear in those still alive. Throughout the Games, the Capitol treats the tributes as commodities; in the form of mutts, they lose any dignity they might have found in death.

As William Davies suggests in *The Limits of Neoliberalism*, what's characteristic of neoliberalism – the especially aggressive form of capitalism that has been advanced for the past 40 years or so – is how it's been argued that these values of competition must be introduced into every sphere of life. Any remaining non-market institution – publicly-provided healthcare where it exists, education, publicly-owned utilities for example – must be made more like markets. But like the Treaty of Treason and everything else that followed, all of this struggles to conceal a contradiction: if selfish individualism and no-holds-barred competition are so natural, why does the Capitol need to spend so much time promoting them?

Chapter 6

"She's a survivor, that one"

"Make sure they remember you"

"I only keep wishing I could think of a way to show the Capitol they don't own me. That I'm more than just a piece in their Games." Peeta makes his plaintive wish on the eve of the Games. It's the limited nature of his hope that's heartbreaking, but he's also being realistic. The arena is inescapable, and so is dying. Given he's not a natural fighter, Peeta is doomed. Katniss too, probably; even though she has some survival skills and reserves of resilience, she faces many far stronger competitors.

Even so, Katniss misunderstands Peeta's point, or in her despair dismisses his hope for dignity: "But you're not. None of us are. That's how the Games work." It's a bitter final conversation between them. The next day in the arena they will be forced to be foes.

The logic of Katniss' view is that the only way not to be owned by the Capitol is to bring down the system, but she knows that's not possible. In hindsight, however, perhaps Peeta's wish plants a seed in her mind, one that comes to fruition in the arena. Or perhaps her bleakness belies her rage at the Capitol. Either way, she'll find a way to show she's more than just a piece in their games, setting off a series of events she couldn't possibly imagine.

"You are stronger than they are"

Despite her pessimism, Katniss has valuable survival skills (inspired by Suzanne Collins' father) and a toughness from her upbringing. So do many of the people from the poorest districts; their revolution will eventually overrun the Capitol and its pampered residents.

This also provides Katniss with some advantage in the Games, even against the career tributes. They may have been prepared pretty much from birth to compete in the Games, trained in martial arts and weapons, and drawing on specialisms from their districts. But they've never been as hungry as Katniss, never had to hunt and forage for food to survive. Their strength and weight would normally be an advantage in combat, but not necessarily in the arena; for example, an underweight Katniss will escape by climbing trees and sleeping in them at night for safety. But this won't be enough.

"I feel like I owe him something, and I hate owing people"

Katniss hates the idea of being seen as weak. It threatens her and her family's survival. Later, with Peeta's surprise declaration of love in the TV interview just before the Games, Katniss is angry because she thinks it makes her look soft. And in the Games themselves, she hides her fear because she thinks it won't be popular with the audience.

Such is her wariness about weakness that Katniss also hates the idea of owing people. At the beginning of the first book, Katniss remembers the first time she encountered Peeta. In scarcity there's a reluctance to be in "debt" to others. This reflects a worry about not being able to pay people back, because we (think we) have little to give in return. Katniss would prefer not to "owe" Peeta for his kindness, starting with the bread he throws her way (told in backstory, and discussed later). Such is her suspicion, she doesn't understand what it means and ponders it like a puzzle, reflecting what she calls the "disbelief of the chronically hungry." Independence and self-sufficiency are familiar and feel safer. But this language of debts also reflects Capitol(ist) thinking: every relationship is a contract.

It has a broader political resonance as well. The debt the districts supposedly owe the Capitol can never be paid; there will never be any release from the sentence imposed on the people of Panem. Instead, Katniss will learn that owing people, mutuality, is not just okay, it's critical.

"What I did was the radical thing"

When Prim "wins" the lottery and Katniss volunteers in her place, the anger of the district toward the Capitol is clear. When the crowd is invited to clap, instead they salute her with three fingers held up – a sign of resistance against the Gamemakers and solidarity with Katniss. Given the dominant ideology of Panem and the Games, it's a revolutionary idea. This gesture will become a symbol of defiance, and later, of revolt. Katniss may not consciously intend it, she says, but it symbolizes the start of her political journey. In a dictatorship, any defiance is inherently radical.

This is the first way in which the Capitol's domination is also its weakness. So pervasive is its propaganda that any diversion from it is magnified. If the Games are a national pageant, the lack of celebration in the districts effectively challenges everything. As Mark Fisher notes in *Capitalist Realism*: "The very oppressive pervasiveness of capitalist realism means that even glimmers of alternative political and economic possibilities can have a disproportionately great effect. The tiniest event can tear a hole in the grey curtain of reaction which has marked the horizons of possibility under capitalist realism. From a situation in which nothing can happen, suddenly anything is possible again."

"We have to stop viewing one another as enemies"

As Mark also notes ("Remember Who the Enemy Is"), Panem's total surveillance society will be turned back on the Capitol. "The personal is political because there is no personal." Katniss' actions during the Games, which are not purposefully revolutionary, will play out in the most public way possible. The TV spectacle of the Games is a national focal point (viewing is mandatory for all of Panem's subjects), but this is what creates such a perfect platform for subversion.

To start with, it allows the districts to begin to relate to each other. In the Games, Katniss befriends a young girl from District 11 called Rue. When they become allies, they learn more about each other's districts than they've ever been taught in school or through Panem's state-controlled media ("It's interesting, hearing about her life. We have so little communication with anyone outside our district"). This begins to bridge the system of segregation: a cross-racial alliance between two of the poorest districts in Panem. Katniss and Rue recognize their common oppression under the power structure. This is not how the game is supposed to be played.

"It's the Capitol I hate, for doing this to all of us"

But then, Rue's death politicizes Katniss, or rather, brings to the surface her buried emotions. It breaks through Katniss' wariness about connections with people. Now, the debt becomes political, the obligation becomes for Katniss to make a statement, to defy the Capitol.

It's also an additional motivation to survive; not just for Katniss to see her family again, her previous private desire, but because it represents a public snub to Panem's rulers. Katniss has to experience her emotions first, though, to begin to release herself from the prison she's created to protect herself. As Alice Miller stated in *Breaking Down the Walls of Silence*, "[I]t is precisely the experience and expression of justifiable anger that gives us the courage to go forward." Katniss will need to feel a lot more anger if she's to take on the Capitol.

Katniss memorializes Rue in a bed of flowers, an act of humanity. Now her actions are conscious: she repeats the solidarity salute from District 12. It's a clear demonstration of defiance: if the Capitol doesn't own her, maybe it doesn't own the districts either. In the film, we cut to a seemingly spontaneous uprising in District 11. The workers destroy machinery and sacks of crops. Peacekeepers rush to snuff out the spark of revolt. But something has started, something that can't be unseen.

"Kind people have a way of working their way inside me and rooting there"

For hours after Rue's death, Katniss walks aimlessly, hoping to run into the career tributes, which would be deadly. As she's about to make camp, a gift arrives, a loaf of bread from District 11. This is unprecedented: a poor district helping a tribute who's not their own. Katniss thinks of the starving people there, pooling their money to give her food, and thanks them aloud. She doesn't know about the disturbances there, of course. But the revolution in collaboration and compassion has begun.

Actually, before the Games, Katniss had started to recognize the significance of small acts of kindness. Peeta tells Katniss what his mother said to him when she came to say goodbye before he's taken off to the Capitol. Peeta's mother remarks that maybe District 12 will finally have a winner, but she means Katniss. "She said, 'She's a survivor, that one.' *She* is." Katniss is taken aback: "Suddenly I'm behind the bakery and I can feel the chill of the rain running down my back, the hollowness in my belly. I sound eleven years old when I speak. "But only because someone helped me."

Katniss may be tough, but it's connecting with others that will save her and start something much bigger.

"The people in this arena weren't crowned for their compassion"

Since we're in the arena, let's talk about games. Game theory is a branch of mathematics that represents "inter-dependent decision-making," situations where the outcomes of one person's decision depends on decisions made by others. It's been applied across social science including politics, as well as in logic, systems science and computer science. Originally, game theory addressed zero-sum games (if I win, you lose, and vice versa). But it can also tell us something about cooperation.

The most well-known model in game theory is the prisoner's dilemma, created by Merrill Flood and Melvin Dresher at the RAND corporation (a think tank famous for its work for the US Department of Defense) in 1950. This demonstrates how two individuals acting in their self-interest can produce an outcome that's bad for both of them. The logical thing for each participant is to choose to protect themself at the expense of the other, but when both participants do this, both suffer. The game explains why two rational individuals might not cooperate, even when it's in their interest to do so.

The Games of *The Hunger Games* are a prisoner's dilemma, designed by the Capitol to crush collaboration. The tributes can form temporary alliances (often the careers initially hunt as a pack), but they know they'll have to kill each other eventually. Similarly, to critics, game theory rationalizes selfish behavior by demonstrating that however we might like to behave, we face stronger incentives to betray each other's trust. Although there are infinite ways in which its models can be designed, game theory appears to have incorporated the assumption that we are naive to hope for cooperation, that hard-wired human nature and the games we play (in the economy, society, politics) just don't work that way.

But it's not true that we're trapped in their games. For example, John Roemer, the American economist and political scientist, has used game theory among other approaches to challenge mainstream economics and consider how we might overcome capitalism. (Revealingly, the idea of cooperation doesn't really exist in most mainstream economic theories, despite evolutionary biologists and anthropologists increasingly viewing Homo sapiens as an essentially cooperative species.) Some of Roemer's more recent work develops a theory of "Kantian optimization" which proposes a rational model for cooperative behavior (*How We Cooperate*). He demonstrates how cooperative behavior can produce the best outcomes for all. Selfish individual behavior is not rational. It's not the only game we can play.

"It's great to have allies as long as you don't have to kill them"

Roemer's approach doesn't depend on assuming that we act like saints; it uses self-interested behavior to suggest how we want and need to cooperate. Cooperation is not the same as altruism: we (can and do) cooperate out of self-interest as well as common interests.

But for this, some degree of trust is often important. In *The Hunger Games*, Katniss establishes trust with Rue, and then with Peeta. She also relies on the career pack betraying each other (they act out of assumptions of self-interest of course).

A key part of Roemer's theory is that we take an action only if we'd prefer a situation in which our actions are universalized, if everyone did the same thing. And if everyone in the Games were like Katniss, Peeta and Rue, this would be true and it would obviously be better. In this sense, it's the career tributes, indoctrinated to believe that the game is good, who are the problem. Nonetheless, the three of them make the first moves and take the risk of establishing trust. And it helps them. Illustrating Roemer's point, Katniss is not a saint, and Peeta and Rue do the logical thing in their self-interest: to try to survive because on paper they're much the weakest competitors.

The point is, it depends on what game we think we're playing. If we're told it's brutally competitive, as the Capitol wants us to believe, then we're more likely to play that way and assume everyone else will too. But Roemer makes a critical point: even though we're told the games of capitalism are like this, many people, maybe most of us, act according to *his* theory. For example, many people choose their occupations based on a desire to contribute to society, not simply for personal enrichment. Mainstream economic theory has stopped us seeing this as clearly as we should: the Capitol's propaganda has tried to conceal the truth that's around us everyday.

"Because that's what you and I do. Protect each other"

We also learn that the kindness and compassion that Katniss demonstrates leads back to before the story starts. Although they both lived in District 12, Katniss and Peeta had never really met. But Peeta did once leave some bread for a starving Katniss. In fact, this was crucial to Katniss' survival ("I had just turned away from Peeta Mellark's bruised face when I saw the dandelion and I knew hope wasn't lost").

The next day, she finally finds the courage to go under the fence that surrounds the district to go hunting. The woods become her family's savior ("That night, we gorged ourselves on dandelion salad and the rest of the bakery bread"), and crucial to Katniss' ability to cope. Survival, even the hope of it, isn't just an individual trait; others can inspire it in us as well.

As noted, Katniss would like to be totally self-reliant; she thinks this is crucial to survival under the system. But she can't be, and *The Hunger Games* is partly the story of how she comes to realize the importance of her interdependence with others. Survival, let alone social change, can't be individual, it has to be collective. It can only happen together.

Such small acts of kindness might seem inconsequential, but they can be the seeds of change. In our political climate, which increasingly rests on the idea that empathy is impossible, kindness might not be a distraction from radical change. Maybe it is radical change.

"You don't forget the face of the person who was your last hope"

Like Roemer, Rebecca Solnit makes this point in her work: we demonstrate non-capitalist values everyday. Solnit has used the example of the mutual help that often emerges after natural disasters to argue that crisis doesn't necessarily mean a nightmarish future (*A Paradise Built in Hell*). But for this, we have to remember not to expect the worst from others, we have to throw off Hobbesian indoctrination.

As Jeremy Adam Smith of the University of California Berkeley Greater Good Science Center suggests, *The Hunger Games* demonstrates a different understanding of our natural inclinations ("Five lessons in human goodness from 'The Hunger Games'", *Berkeley Blog*, 25 April 2012), including: the psychological and biological roots of compassion, empathy and cooperation; killing is against human nature; wealth makes us less compassionate; people are motivated to help others by empathy, not reason or numbers; real power flows from social and emotional intelligence, not strength and viciousness (Peeta particularly demonstrates this); and social connections trump power and independence.

The war of all against all within the arena is meant to reveal the worst in humanity. But ultimately the Capitol's Games will fail.

"It's not a mistake to go on living"

The ripples keep spreading: Rue helping Katniss; Katniss memorializing Rue; the gift from District 11; Peeta saving Katniss from the career tributes; Katniss caring for Peeta when he's injured; Thresh, who's from District 11, saving Katniss from another competitor because she was kind to Rue. Katniss and Thresh understand that they've broken the rules of the game, at least temporarily, that they may be forced to fight each other later. But that's for later.

This begins to model how we build the trust that Roemer says is essential to a different kind of game. It depends on how long we think the game lasts. In his influential and intriguing book *Finite and Infinite Games*, James Carse describes how there are two main types of games: finite games are about competition, but infinite games are about cooperation.

As Carse summarizes it:

> A finite game is played for the purpose of winning, an infinite game for the purpose of continuing the play. Finite games are those instrumental activities – from sports to politics to wars – in which the participants obey rules, recognize boundaries and announce winners and losers. The infinite game...includes any authentic interaction...that changes rules, plays with boundaries and exists solely for the purpose of continuing the game. A finite player seeks power; the infinite one displays self-sufficient strength. Finite games are theatrical, necessitating an audience; infinite ones are dramatic, involving participants.

The power in this idea is that the game we think we're playing changes how we play. Is it a finite game of winners and losers, or an infinite game which offers many more possibilities? Finite games may offer wealth and status, but infinite games offer something more subtle but potentially much grander. The Hunger Games are designed as a finite game. Katniss and Peeta begin to turn it into an infinite one. They care for each other, as if the game isn't going to end. Katniss knows there's an audience, but she starts to act authentically. They display different strengths to those the Capitol wants: not seeking the glory of victory, but hoping to change the rules completely.

But it's difficult. Fear, separation, selfishness – these are inherent to the games the Capitol designs. They co-opt us, we feel like we have no choice. Which is why, in reaction to Katniss planting the seeds of solidarity, the Gamemakers ensure it's impossible to win the Games this way. They have to change the rules to create confrontation. For example, as noted, when toward the end of the Games the Gamemakers announce that there are supplies that the remaining tributes need at the cornucopia, they're trying to engineer another bloodbath between the districts.

But once we notice it, again here the Capitol has a weakness. In making the Games so unwinnable, that even if you "win" you suffer grief and trauma, the Gamemakers encourage their subversion. Why not defy the Capitol? What have we got to lose?

"I want to start an uprising"

Is Katniss apolitical, lacking in class consciousness? It seems that way at the start. But as discussed, she's numbed and can't see how the Capitol can be challenged. However, experiencing the excess of the Capitol and the horror of the Games, she's radicalized, at last allowing herself to feel anger at Panem's elite. Battling for survival in the arena, but trying to act with compassion where she can, she begins to represent something else: a determination to demonstrate a different set of values. Paradoxically, her pessimism about the possibility of escape will lead her to challenge the system in a particularly powerful way.

This is also why Katniss has become an icon for so many young people; she appears apolitical at first, because she can't envisage the possibility of change, and there are no forms of political activity that the system would respond to anyway. But their disillusionment masks a deep anger at injustice, corruption and exploitation. They think differently from the Capitol. And when survival is at stake, they will demonstrate their defiance.

Something that unites the diverse, proliferating protest movements led by young people in our age – from Black Lives Matter to the Never Again agenda for gun control, the school climate strike campaign to the Sunrise movement – is their underlying focus on survival, collective human survival. Because they operate outside of traditional party structures and in open and participative ways, they've been characterized as lacking ideology. But like Katniss, they're defiant, act with solidarity and are led by compassion. And their analyses are blunt: "reform" isn't enough, the system needs to change for there to be justice, fairness and a chance to live.

"I can find you. I can reach you. Perhaps I am watching you now"

Another symbol of subversion, another way that Katniss turns the Capitol's systems against it, is the Mockingjay. This bird, and Katniss, will become the symbols of the revolution.

Containment requires surveillance. As reality TV, the Games are filmed from every angle. But the districts too are closely monitored. Before the arena Katniss assumes they're being watched, which makes her wary about what she says. In *Catching Fire*, President Snow knows she used to escape into the woods, but she doesn't know how. It doesn't really matter; the power of totalitarian regimes is that they make you assume someone is always watching.

During the first rebellion, the Capitol bred a series of genetically altered animals as weapons. One was a bird called a jabberjay that could memorize and repeat human conversations. But the rebels used them to feed the Capitol disinformation, so the birds were abandoned to die off in the wild. Only they didn't die off, they mated with mockingbirds to produce mockingjays, a new species that could replicate human melodies. As Katniss recognizes, mockingjays represent a failure by the Capitol, a dent in its invulnerability. Just by their survival, they mock its rule.

The mockingjays also become a tool in the arena. Rue explained to Katniss how the residents of District 11 use the mockingjays to communicate. Katniss and Rue use them to coordinate their survival against the career tributes. After Rue is killed, Katniss hears the mockingjays still singing her song and they become a reminder of her, of the possibility of solidarity. The memory also hardens Katniss' hatred of the Capitol and her desire to rebel.

The jabberjays of our world are Google, Amazon, Facebook... Not only do they try to monitor our every move, they've helped governments to spy illegally on citizens. In the future, under capitolism, justified by "national security," they will be the greatest tools any authoritarian could hope for. We need to find our own ways to subvert the surveillance state, to turn its tools back on itself, or be forever watching what we say and even dare to think.

"This is the time to show them everything. Make sure they remember you"

Before the Games, in the ceremony in the Capitol's City Circle, Peeta surprises Katniss by grabbing her hand and holding it aloft, a sign of district pride but which also represents them as a couple. In the interviews before the Games, Peeta shocks everyone by declaring his love for Katniss. But she distrusts his motives – the corrosive effect of reality TV on its "contestants" – and as noted, she's annoyed that this might make her look weak.

But when the survivors are down to six, Katniss joins forces with Peeta. And when she treats him for his injuries, for the first time she also plays up the romance, albeit awkwardly, recognizing that it could be crucial to their survival as a source of new sponsors. Katniss approaches it somewhat cynically, but she's also confused in her own mind. It's still subverting the Capitol, though, providing a different story for the audience than the Gamemakers intend, changing the game.

"It must be very fragile, if a handful of berries can bring it down"

Unseen by Katniss and Peeta, there's clearly been a strong

reaction to the star-crossed lovers storyline by the audience in the Capitol. The Gamemakers are forced to respond with a change in the rules: two tributes from the same district can win the Games together. It's a crack in the supposedly impregnable state of nature. The tributes have demonstrated their power, no longer just subjects in the story but also its actors.

The Gamemakers try to assimilate and depoliticize fraternity and cooperation into a sentimental story, into Katniss and Peeta's "love alliance." This might suggest the impossibility of defeating the Capitol, but really it underlines its weakness. They too are subject to public opinion. For a totalitarian regime, it's a painful admission.

Ironically, or perhaps proving the point, some commentary and media coverage of the series focused on the Katniss-Peeta-Gale love triangle, distracting from other, more meaningful reasons why young people respond to the story both politically and personally. But then, who cares what the Capitol tries to make us think?

"They have to have their victor"

But the games aren't over. The Gamemakers revoke their rule change: now there can be only one victor. The defiance can't be allowed to continue. Katniss and Peeta fight back, in the only way that their powerlessness allows, their final act of subversion. Peeta throws away his knife first and urges Katniss to shoot him. But Katniss knows that the Capitol needs a victor, and the only way to deny them is...for both of them to commit suicide.

There'll be no winners this year, no victory parade, no normalization of brutality. An empty podium, the audience forced to think of the children who never returned from the arena. The story of the Games as national unifier will be broken, its toll of savagery underlined.

As Mark Fisher suggests ("Remember Who the Enemy Is"): "This is Katniss's decisive step into becoming a revolutionary, and in choosing death, she wins back her life – or the possibility of a life no longer lived as a slave-subordinate, but as a free individual."

"I will die, in my own small way, undefeated"

In his book *Domination and the Arts of Resistance*, James C. Scott describes how confrontations between the powerless and powerful are laden with deception. Peasants, serfs, slaves, laborers and prisoners are not free to speak their minds in the presence of power. The powerless feign deference and the powerful assert their mastery. Although the powerful seek to make this public transcript seem inevitable, the subordinate understands it's constructed. But sometimes, the powerless shift the relationship by openly challenging the narrative. This final, explosive shift Scott calls the "rupture," when both the message and the messenger are no longer disguised. The mask is taken off.

For the subordinate, this is risky, long overdue, but liberating. It's a moment of personal authentication, a recapturing of dignity, of the truth that no one can legitimately rule another.

While the dominant will seek to recapture power, the subordinate has changed forever. For the dominant, it's an uprising that has come out of nowhere and is interpreted as rebellion.

Katniss and Peeta's decision is paradoxical: victory in defeat, a statement of power and powerlessness at once. Katniss has finally realized her true anger against the cruelty of the Capitol, and after so long watching what she says, makes an authentic, public statement of non-compliance. She turns her hopelessness back against the system; she also breaks through the desensitizing effect of reality TV by providing a genuinely shocking moment.

This type of protest has a long history, of those who have sacrificed themselves as a symbol against the unconscionable. Collins, a fan of classical stories, may also have thought of

Spartacus, the gladiator who was a leader in the Third Servile War, a major slave uprising against the Roman Republic. Little is known about him beyond the events of the war, but in the 1960 Stanley Kubrick film at least, before Spartacus and his fellow rebels are crucified he states that: "Death is the only freedom a slave knows...That's why we'll win."

"Because of her, they all think they're invincible"

The Gamemakers are forced to back down. Both Katniss and Peeta are allowed to survive the Games – the winning tributes of District 12.

Katniss tells herself that she was just trying to keep them both alive, that any rebellion was incidental. But the defiance was there all along, it just wasn't so public. Katniss and Gale's illegal hunting. The Hob, the bustling black market of District 12. The collective gesture of respect from the residents of her district after Katniss volunteers as tribute. The ceremony, with Cinna's costumes representing a proud District 12. Katniss challenging the Gamemakers during the training session. The mockingjays. Peeta's desire to retain his identity in the Games. Katniss focusing on survival rather than slaying her opponents. Katniss tenderly memorializing Rue. And Katniss and Peeta's final act of subversive submission.

But power hates being challenged. Such actions will not go unpunished. Far from being free, to the extent that any victors can ever be, Katniss has now entered the political arena, and the stakes have just become even greater.

The first part of the story ends ominously. President Snow crowns the victors and remarks about Katniss' Mockingjay pin. He recognizes the threat, more than she does. As Haymitch warns her: "You're in trouble. Word is the Capitol's furious about you showing them up in the arena. The one thing they can't stand is being laughed at, and they're the joke of Panem."

Part III

The Revolution

Chapter 7

"Fire is catching"

"We can't go back"

The Hunger Games is the story of how a revolution happens. In *Catching Fire,* the second part of the story, despite gathering dissent against the system, the Capitol strikes back and appears to have found ways to manage the revolt. But in the final part, *Mockingjay,* the revolution takes flight and the real fight for the future of Panem has begun.

As Mark Fisher suggests ("Remember Who The Enemy Is"), perhaps the most remarkable thing about the series is how it presupposes that revolution is necessary: "The problems are logistical, not ethical, and the issue is simply how and when revolution can be made to happen, not if it should happen at all."

It turns out that there is an organized rebellion, hidden underground. We're taken into its heart. *The Hunger Games,* a hugely popular young adult series, surprisingly ends up centering on revolutionary politics and tactics. Mass dissent is vital, but, the story suggests, it's not enough. We need serious structures to survive the Capitol, let alone to storm its citadel.

But there's a tension, played out in the series: can these structures be reconciled with a much more open, instinctive, humane revolution in values – one that much more closely matches the authentic thinking of today's young people – in a way that successfully challenges the Capitol's domination over us? Can we win the war against power?

"If it were up to me, I would try to forget the Hunger Games entirely"

Catching Fire starts with Katniss and Peeta facing the "Victory

Tour" of the districts, which will culminate in a ceremony in their own district. In the Games, Katniss thinks that survival might mean freedom. Now she'll come to understand what Haymitch meant when he said that there are no winners.

Following a menacing meeting with President Snow, a terrible threat looms over her. The only defense that might avoid the Capitol's retribution is that she was so in love with Peeta she couldn't bear to be without him. Cruelly, having revealed her anger toward the Capitol, she has to retreat. It's containment again. But what choice does she have?

However, at the start of the tour, Peeta expresses solidarity with District 11 by pledging one month of their winnings to the tributes' families every year. When it's Katniss' turn to speak, she recalls her relationship with Rue, but she falters…Then, from somewhere in the crowd, someone – it turns out to be an old man – whistles Rue's four-note Mockingjay tune. And suddenly, in unison, in what must have been coordinated, everyone in the crowd presses the three middle fingers of their left hand against their lips and extends them to Katniss.

Peacekeepers charge into the crowd, drag the old man up onto the platform and shoot him. It's a disturbing demonstration of the Capitol's determination to crush dissent.

Katniss is in a horrendous position. In spite of her experience in the Games and her growing political consciousness, she must remain compliant to the Capitol. Now even her existence represents a threat.

"They don't take these things lightly"

The Capitol is so quick to act because its leaders recognize its rule is fragile. Of course, that's not how President Snow justifies the need for the Capitol to keep control. He makes the Hobbesian argument, that uprisings lead to revolution and civil war.

"It must be very fragile, if a handful of berries can bring it down," Katniss comments, in her characteristically cautious sarcasm. Snow pauses, then responds, "It is fragile, but not in the way that you suppose." It's not clear what he's referring to. The Capitol can manage disobedience; its control of Katniss is one example of that, as are its demonstrations of how it deals with defiance. No, more likely it refers to the existence of a more serious threat to the Capitol's rule, one that at this point Katniss is unaware of.

After the old man is murdered, Haymitch tells Katniss and Peeta to go along with the scripted tour and do what they're told. But in hindsight, he might have another motive. "What about them? Who protects them?", he asks, referring to the ordinary people of the districts. It's an unusually conscientious question coming from the cynical former tribute. But if he's referring to timing, it makes sense: don't cause trouble unless you can take down the Capitol.

This is the question we face. The Capitol can crush dissent. It can characterize disorder as acting against the common good and divide protesters against the public. Or even assimilate them, as with Katniss and Peeta's symbolic challenge in the Games. What it's far more wary about, as Snow suggests, is the spark that's followed by a much more organized challenge.

"This is what President Snow calls an uprising"

To prove the point, increasing protests mean greater state repression. Early on in *Catching Fire,* Katniss glimpses a news report, one she's not supposed to see. Riots are breaking out in District 8, one of the more rebellious areas. Katniss later learns that the revolt was organized and started on the evening of Katniss and Peeta's Victory Tour visit. It's put down by the Capitol, but clearly things are getting out of control. There are rumors of other uprisings in Districts 7 and 11. Later, Katniss hears about "production backups" affecting other districts...

Even in District 12, usually one of the most quiescent, the Capitol sends in harsher Peacekeepers and a new Head

Peacekeeper. The mines are closed, there are food shortages, the residents are starving. Are the people of Panem prepared for this?

"In the Capitol, you're the one they're scared of now"

And then, a critical exchange between President Snow and Plutarch Heavensbee about how the Capitol should deal with this growing challenge. Snow dismisses Katniss ("She's not who they think she is. She's not a leader. She just wants to save her own skin"), and in a sense he's right, she has typically been more concerned about her and her family's security than public matters. But he also recognizes that she's become a beacon of hope for the rebellion. She must be eliminated.

Heavensbee agrees that Katniss should die, "but in the right way, at the right time." Plutarch says first she needs to be undermined, and that, "We need to show that she's one of us." Presumably he means selfish, concerned only with her own survival. Heavensbee proposes squeezing the districts even more: "Shut down the black markets, take away what little they have, then double the amount of floggings and executions. Put them on TV, broadcast them live, sow fear, more fear..." He suggests linking Katniss to increasing repression: the more she's trivialized by the Capitol, the more the ordinary people of Panem should suffer.

Snow thinks it's a brilliant plan. But, it turns out, it's exactly what the regime shouldn't do. And as we'll see, Heavensbee might have other motives for proposing it.

"I am going back into the arena"

Every 25 years there's a special Hunger Games, the Quarter Quell. Snow makes a shocking announcement: the tributes will be drawn from previous winners of the Games. Perhaps he doesn't think Heavensbee's plan is cruel enough. His plan will re-write Katniss' subversion, her demonstration of cooperation and compassion, and eradicate any hope. Either she'll be killed, ridding the Capitol of the symbol of the rebellion, or she'll kill the most popular celebrities in Panem, severing the growing solidarity between the districts.

But the Capitol miscalculates. In the interviews the night before the Games, the tributes exploit their fame to make the audience question the Games, perhaps for the first time. These are not just the othered poor of the districts; in the Capitol they're thought of as friends. Katniss' wedding dress transforms into the Mockingjay. Peeta supercharges the storyline about their relationship by claiming that Katniss is pregnant, sending the audience into a frenzy. And as the anthem plays, the tributes hold hands in unity (of course, Katniss started it, with her alliance with Rue in the 74th Games). The television pictures are cut off, but not in time. Everyone in Panem has seen this display of defiance.

"Ladies and gentlemen, let the 75th Hunger Games begin!"

Katniss realizes she must find a way to fight for the rebellion. Like the districts, she hasn't got much left to lose. But she's focused on saving Peeta, who she believes is able to express more eloquently the challenge to the Capitol, and because she thinks he's a better person.

What Katniss doesn't know is that she's already part of the rebellion. In the arena, echoing her willingness to sacrifice herself for Peeta, many of the tributes are dedicated to keeping her alive. Ironically, given the previous Games, Katniss misses the collaboration going on all around her. Despite Haymitch's advice to "remember who the real enemy is," she doesn't trust the other tributes and muses on who she will have to fight to ensure that Peeta survives. At one point, she even senses that the other tributes are also trying to save Peeta, but why?

However, eventually it's Katniss, the Mockingjay, who's

rescued from the arena (an arena which may have been designed to be escapable...more of which in a moment). She's taken to a part of Panem everyone thinks has been destroyed, and into the heart of revolution.

"Thirteen? There's no Thirteen. It got blown off the map"

Katniss is taken to District 13, the revolutionary underground. She complains it took them a long time to act ("Why haven't they helped us?"). But Gale, who has joined the rebellion, defends them: "They had to build up a rebel base in the Capitol, get some sort of underground organized in the districts…Then they needed someone to set the whole thing in motion. They needed you."

Before the Dark Days there was already a substantial underground facility in the district, built over centuries as a clandestine refuge for government leaders in time of war or a last resort for humanity if life above ground became unlivable. This was also the center of Panem's nuclear weapons development, the Capitol's primary military-industrial manufacturer.

But during the Dark Days, District 13 was one of the major forces of the rebellion. It wrestled control from the Peacekeepers, trained nuclear missiles on the Capitol, then struck a deal: it would play dead in exchange for being left alone. The Capitol couldn't attack 13 without certain retaliation. It was forced to accept the proposal.

In the 75 years since, the district's population retreated to bunkers. New construction continued underground. The Capitol demolished the visible remains of the district and cut off access from outside. Perhaps the Capitol assumed that, without help, District 13 would die off. It almost did a few times, but always managed to pull through by strict sharing of resources, strenuous discipline and constant vigilance against any attacks from the Capitol.

"This is the revolution, and you are the Mockingjay"

On a closer reading, the revolution may have been in motion from the very beginning. Before the 74th Games, Cinna and Haymitch direct Katniss and Peeta to present themselves as a pair, despite her obvious reluctance. Then Cinna matches costumes for them in the opening ceremony ("Just the perfect touch of rebellion") and instructs them to hold hands. Cinna volunteered as stylist to District 12's tributes, which was unusual given the district's poor reputation. And Haymitch demands that they're at each others' side and act amiably whenever they're in public, then plots with Peeta before he declares his love for Katniss in the pre-Games interview.

In the book of *The Hunger Games*, it's Madge, the mayor's daughter in District 12, who gives Katniss her gold Mockingjay pin, with "an urgency about her tone" that surprises Katniss ("Promise you'll wear it into the arena, Katniss?" she asks. "Promise?"). And then just before the 74th Games begin, Cinna fastens the pin, which Katniss had forgotten about, to her costume. He does the same thing before the Quarter Quell, just before he is killed by Peacekeepers; clearly, the Capitol has had enough of his insubordination, or perhaps suspects he's with the rebels. He'd also designed Katniss' fiery Mockingjay dress for the interview ("Nothing Cinna designs is arbitrary"). And after the first Games, someone returns the Mockingjay pin to Katniss's room; just as a momento, or a message, that her role in promoting dissent isn't over just yet?

And then the second Games, the Quarter Quell, with an arena designed by Plutarch Heavensbee, which could be sabotaged by a group of experienced competitors...Katniss is angry because she was unaware of the plot. But given her initial hopelessness, would she have participated in it if she had been aware? It's possible that the leaders of District 13 spotted the emergence of a symbol for their revolution way back when Katniss volunteered for the Games in place of her sister. Here was someone with courage and integrity and the perfect touch of rebellious spirit, someone who could act as a figurehead. We learn that Heavensbee has for several years been part of an undercover group plotting to overthrow the Capitol; as a Gamemaker with a keen eye for storytelling, he would have seen how important Katniss could become. So they steered her and Peeta toward subverting the Games. Katniss did the rest, with a little help from Haymitch orchestrating sponsors (perhaps also supporters of the revolution) back in the Capitol.

"We can take down the Capitol"

So, there are two revolutions: the spontaneous public one in which Katniss emerges organically as a symbol of district defiance; and the carefully plotted private one, orchestrated by a dedicated underground cell with the resources required for success.

In turn, there are two ways of thinking about how revolutions come about, two lessons for our world. The first is that exploitative regimes are destined to collapse. Cruelty and containment can't last forever. Eventually, the masses will rise up; they have little left to lose, and the skills they've learned from surviving under the regime will ensure their success.

Further, power is psychological. Regimes rely on terror to repress their people. But at some point, living with fear becomes exhausting; when we're too tired to be afraid anymore, or when other things take precendence, there's no going back. As with individuals, there's a breaking point when our coping mechanisms can't bear any more. We realize we have the power we need, we've had it all along. In this way, revolutions can seem to happen at speed; once a supposedly impregnable regime starts to falter and is shown not to be in control of events, when their propaganda starts to crumble, suddenly the ground gives way.

The second view is that this is rarely enough. They may lead to occassional outbreaks of dissent, but these can be managed by any adequately adept regime. Such disobedience can even be useful to elites in suggesting the "anarchy" that revolution would bring. Instead, revolutions happen because networks have formed, plans made, resources gathered.

Two things are critical. First, every oppressive regime has its ambivalent insiders, those who accept its rule because they are relatively well-positioned and receive privileges. When these elites stop obeying the regime, its pillars of support start to crack. These insiders know how the regime works, where its strategic vulnerabilities are, and how it can be brought down. Second, any revolution needs to be deadly serious. In Panem, there'd already been a failed first rebellion against the Capitol. The leaders of District 13 are well aware of the consequences of a second disaster. The campaign against the Capitol will have only one chance.

"This is what they do! And we must fight back!"

In our world, we need both. *The Hunger Games* is a good dramatization of why this is.

The new protest movements, whether explicitly of the left or not, can be very good at the spontaneous, the rapid mass mobilization to support a cause or highlight a hypocrisy, especially online. They use symbols creatively and effectively, including from popular entertainment. They have a strong attachment to natural fairness and justice, and to solidarity. They're brave and resourceful. Generationally, tempermentally, emotionally, they're Katniss.

But because of their disgust and disillusionment with existing structures of power and politics, because they're often more naturally anarchistic (something we'll come back to in the next chapter), they can lack worked out plans and strategies for how to take power. After all, they see power used corruptly and cruelly all around them; no wonder they're wary of it.

But a real rebellion needs a real plan for power, how the Capitol will react to being challenged, and how on earth its control can ever be brought down. Katniss has no plan for bringing down the Capitol either, she can't even begin to envisage it. Of course, the capitols of our world have no such reservations about power; they cling to it and use it to entrench their wealth and influence, and will do until it's ripped out of their hands. They fight for it.

"You might want to experiment with some warmth"

In *The Hunger Games*, a rebellion is underway, in secret at first, exploiting the dissent that Katniss sparks as an authentic symbol of defiance, and then publically, using her as the figurehead of the revolution. Soon, most of the districts join the fight against the Capitol.

But the rebellion does something that the left doesn't do enough: use familiar symbols and meanings, including from popular culture, to draw people into revolt (the Games are a reality TV show after all). The leaders of the second rebellion didn't create the symbol and meaning of this popular revolt (perhaps), but they do seize on it effectively.

Like many despotic regimes in real life, the Capitol will do anything to hold onto power, including destroying District 12, Katniss' home, and bombing civilians into submission. But District 13's organization has enabled it to survive. It's a hierarchically-controlled, highly disciplined revolutionary vanguard, led by President Alma Coin, who seeks to succeed Snow as the leader of Panem. Decision-making is kept to Coin's small group of advisers, although she does have to keep her district on side by persuading them of the wisdom of her decisions.

The district is rigid in its thinking and resistant to change. It's strict and spartan. Everyone wears the same gray uniform and sleeps in identical living quarters. They're given a temporary tattoo of their personalized schedule for the day (Katniss ignores it). They're thrifty and ration food carefully; waste is frowned upon. Even a small deviation from sharing is met with detention. But education is free and refugees can become citizens, apparently in part because the district needs more genetic diversity due to a deadly virus some years before.

But there's no joy, celebration or art (what are we fighting for again?). Katniss even needs permission to keep the family cat. Weddings are not celebrated since marriages are done through a simple signing; Finnick Odair and Annie Cresta are the exception, but even this is done for propaganda purposes. As Katniss thinks, "In some ways, District 13 is even more controlling than the Capitol."

"All I have to do is play my part"

Katniss is ambivalent about District 13. The fight against the Capitol requires leadership, structure and discipline. But the district hardly represents the seeds of a better world. As Kantiss recognizes, it reflects the Capitol more than it should.

She's escaped the arena and the clutches of the Capitol, but as ever, she's being used, packaged and presented, her agency taken away. She's a symbol, but not taken seriously. Katniss may not be deliberately depoliticized anymore, as the Capitol tried to do with her, but neither is she respected as a legitimate political actor by the rebellion, despite her obvious bravery, instincts, intelligence and fortitude.

In story terms, it's possible to be frustrated with Katniss through much of *The Hunger Games*, particulary her reluctance to be a revolutionary, even to act as a symbol for the revolution. She's faced with an obviously odious regime; usually as audiences we have little patience with passive characters. Of course, we like her because she's principled, brave and resourceful in so many other ways. But Katniss is also wise. She knows the cost of conflict. She's covered with the scars of violence and trauma. She's wary of whether the conflict that she's become a symbol of, however important, is likely to result in further harm and loss.

Later, the Capitol tries to use Katniss' concerns against her. When they capture, torture and brainwash Peeta, they get him to call out to her on television: "Katniss...how do you think this will end? What will be left? No one is safe. Not in the Capitol. Not in the districts." But Katniss needs to be reminded that, "You haven't hurt people – you've given them an opportunity. They just have to be brave enough to take it."

"That seems to be crossing some kind of line"

Unlike some other Hollywood movies, *The Hunger Games* doesn't romanticize rebellion. Films typically relish war and conflict, but this series takes the costs and consequences seriously. District 13 is a militarized community. Everyone over the age of 14 is addressed as "soldier." Like Panem under the Capitol's rule, violence and domination run through its political culture, even if it is for a better purpose. Remember that the corrupting nature of militarism is a core theme for Suzanne Collins. The third part of the story in particular explores the morality of war and conflict through Katniss' ambivalence. It also provides clues to the meaning of the Mockingjay revolution (discussed in the next chapter).

Katniss is disturbed by Gale's willingness to kill as the rebels fight District 2. Gale thinks he's on her side, or at least on the side of the Mockingjay revolution, that he's taking down an evil system. In fact, Katniss fears, he's perpetuating the larger problem, that of war itself. By the end of the story, the difference between Gale's stance and Katniss' core beliefs ends any possibility of a relationship between them.

There's also the implication that District 13 has also engaged in the torture and punishment of political prisoners, spies, and traitors, which appalls Katniss. In the end, she'll realize what the rebellion is capable of, how its leaders think in many of the same ways as the Capitol. Snow's regime is horrific. But what she's trying to overthrow can't just be one regime. It has to be any system that's founded on violence, any regime that believes people are expendable.

"No one who supports the Capitol is innocent"

Although Suzanne Collins hasn't done that many interviews about the series, she has emphasized the importance of her concerns around "just war" and how these are at the center of her story ("Suzanne Collins Talks About 'The Hunger Games', the Books and the Movies", *The New York Times*, 18 October 2018):

> Just-war theory has evolved over thousands of years in an attempt to define what circumstances give you the moral right to wage war and what is acceptable behavior within that war and its aftermath...In *The Hunger Games* Trilogy, the districts rebel against their own government because of its corruption. The citizens of the districts have no basic human rights, are treated as slave labor, and are subjected to the Hunger Games annually. I believe the majority of today's audience would define that as grounds for revolution. They have just cause but the nature of the conflict raises a lot of questions.

As Collins explains, Peeta and Gale represent not so much two points on a love triangle, more two perspectives in the just war debate. Gale, because of his experiences and temperament, tends toward the legitimacy of violence. Peeta's inclination is toward diplomacy. Katniss isn't just deciding on a partner, she's figuring out her worldview. Collins avoids easy answers, though. The rebellion eventually triumphs, the Capitol falls, but its means are questioned and questionable, especially in the final twist to the tale.

Contrary to Hobbesian hopelessness, to Collins, "Obviously, we're not in a position at the moment for the eradication of war to seem like anything but a far-off dream. But at one time, the eradication of slave markets in the United States seemed very far off...We can change...It's not simple, and it's a very long and drawn-out process, but you can hope." (Rick Margolis, "The last battle: With Mockingjay on its way, Suzanne Collins weighs in on Katniss and the Capitol", *School Library Journal*, August 2010).

"Tonight, turn your weapons to the Capitol"

Eventually, Katniss decides to play the role of the Mockingjay, to, as she puts it dryly, "become the best-dressed rebel in history." Katniss has been pressured into playing two roles by two sides, the star-crosed lover and then the rebel leader. She's naturally neither, but in the climatic moment of *Mockingjay* she'll assert her authenticity and reveal her true position. That's still to come, however.

For the moment, Katniss remains ambivalent about the conflict. There's some interesting gender politics around conflict and violence. Peeta's ethics challenge traditional gender norms. He's not the typical aggressive male, particularly compared to Gale. But neither is Katniss merely gender swapped; she's prepared to fight, but she wants the war to be just.

Echoing her actions in the arena, Katniss rejects the idea of winning at any price. She hates the games she's forced to play and the cost in human lives. We aren't used to heroes like this. We've been indoctrinated by a thousand films and stories, centered on male protagonists, in which violence is the easy solution. Heroes are supposed to use strength to dominate their opponents. But such stories, even if nominally on the side of right, end up promoting the same value system that causes cruelty in the first place. And of course, Katniss knows what that feels like, in the Capitol's Games and its exploitation of the districts. What's she's trying to hold onto is not being corrupted by the same values that have caused so much damage.

The same goes for the rebellion in practice. Some people seem to look forward to a revolutionary conflict revolving around power, strength and violence. Either these romantics haven't experienced violence and trauma, or they don't anticipate being in the arena anyway.

"While you live, the revolution lives"

The revolution can't survive if we don't. In collapse, District 13 might be our future, those of us not within the Capitol's walls: a revolutionary underground focused on survival, until maybe, some time later, we might challenge the Capitol once again. By necessity, the district maintains its own livestock and vegetable farms to survive after the Capitol destroyed everything above ground; these are concealed so as not to arouse suspicion in the other districts. District 13 is a metaphor, or maybe even a model: self-contained communities that enable us to survive outside of a corrupt, cruel, collapsing system.

District 13 is a vanguard revolutionary movement. It represents a united working-class party, the hope of some traditional socialist thinking. But in another way it challenges some of this traditional thinking.

For example, Nick Srnicek and Alex Williams (*Inventing the Future*) characterize much left-wing thinking in the West since the 1960s as "folk politics," aiming to bring politics down to the human scale via personal involvement in direct action, and a focus on single issues and localism. But to Srnicek and Williams, these are insufficient to tackle global capitalism and neoliberalism. We've abandoned strategy, universalism, abstraction and the hard work of building workable global alternatives to capitalism. Jodi Dean (*The Communist Horizon*) has equally remarked that "Goldman Sachs doesn't care if you raise chickens." She suggests that any dissidence which can't be generalized and abstracted is doomed. The "retreat" to the local, the emphasis on resilience, the rejection of the universal and the systemic – these are regarded as representing surrender in the struggle against (the) Capitol.

But there's a reason to focus on building alternative communites now. In collapse our current systems of industrial agriculture and global trade will break down. The local, horizontal, human scale and communal will be critical to our survival. We'll need greater self-sufficiency and stronger communities, to escape our dependency on the Capitol. And doing so would be a good thing in itself.

"There's so many things we should discuss"

This is a chance to begin to build new worlds: new structures, services, networks. Building our own infrastructure is rebellion. Decentralized renewable energy, food, democracy, welfare, health services. Worker-run cooperatives, direct democracy popular assemblies, voluntary federations of small polities, mutual aid networks, community land trusts. All of these could create a very different kind of society than the one pushed by the Capitol. A practical utopian vision of an ecological society beyond war, domination and scarcity.

This radical decentralization would be safer, more resilient, not backward-looking but the best way to prepare for the future. Guerrilla communities, not so much protesting against the system but progressively leaving it, seceding from capitolist structures, systems and control.

Even food banks, now representative of the failure of our economies to provide for people, could be an important part of how communities survive, even begin to thrive again, expanded to grow food and promote local food sovereignty compared to the corporate food system. All based on solidarity, mutual support, cooperation, love. It's maybe our only chance of winning the hunger games.

This localism negates the logic of unbridled capitalism/capitolism. Call it socialist survivalism. As Natalie Osborne has put it ("For still possible cities: a politics of failure for the politically depressed", *Australian Geographer*, Volume 50, Issue 2,

2019), this rejects "the fantasy of an elsewhere...a rejection of the cruel optimism of a post-revolutionary-utopian-World-on-her-way...We failed to save The World, but there are other, subaltern worlds here, accessible if we attend and care for them."

"Fear does not work when there is hope"

Like Katniss, we don't want to be stuck in a suffocating District 13. What's at stake is how we survive and start to build better worlds in the context of collapse, authoritarianism and fear.

The difference between Katniss and District 13 is between an older tradition of socialist-Marxist-statist thought and action, and a young generation's emerging survivalism, supported by a "new" set of values: anti-hierarchy, humaneness, values, openness, compassion, diversity. As George Orwell wrote, "the job of the thinking person is not to reject socialism but to make up his mind to humanise it."

Neither the Capitol nor District 13.

Chapter 8

"Just you remember who the real enemy is"

"You're not afraid of fire, are you, Katniss?"

The iconic covers of the three *Hunger Games* books depict the Mockingjay, the symbol of the revolution. In the first image, the bird is contained in a circle, possibly representing the Game arena or the Capitol's system of confinement. The second depicts the bird, now on fire, beginning to spread its wings. In the third, the bird is taking flight.

In myth, birds have traditionally been symbols of power and freedom. The theft of fire to benefit humanity is another recurring theme in many world mythologies. The origin of fire is often depicted as a little bird bearing on its tail a red mark, the mark of fire. In many cases the fire is stolen. This also recalls the phoenix, the powerful, mystical bird. After a long life, it dies in a fire of its own making, only to rise again from the ashes.

In *Fahrenheit 451*, one of Suzanne Collins' favorite novels, the phoenix is of course a symbol of rebirth, but also resistance. After the city is reduced to ashes by bombers (in *The Hunger Games*, the Capitol also terrorizes the districts using bombers), Granger, the leader of a group of wandering intellectual exiles who memorize books to preserve their contents, compares human beings and the phoenix. Both destroy themselves in fire. Both start again amid the ashes. If people keep books, which preserve the past and allow people to learn the lessons of prior tragedies, Granger hopes that humanity will remember the suffering caused by destruction and avoid destroying itself in the future.

Panem has caught fire. War rages between the rebels and the Capitol. But does the Mockingjay revolution really represent the rebirth of society, or something else?

"Ladies and gentlemen, welcome to the 76th Hunger Games"

We mentioned the story of Spartacus and its influence on *The Hunger Games* in Chapter 6. Suzanne Collins has also referred to it (Lev Grossman, "'I was destined to write a gladiator game': A conversation with Suzanne Collins and Francis Lawrence", *Time*, 20 November 2013):

> There's a basis for the war, historically, in the Hunger Games, which would be the third servile war, which was Spartacus's war, where you have a man who is a slave who is then turned into a gladiator who broke out of the gladiator school and led a rebellion and then became the face of the war. So there is a historical precedent for that arc for a character.

Katniss is persuaded to become the face of the rebellion, and it takes her symbolic name, the Mockingjay revolution. The final part of the series depicts this revolution. As the rebel unit Katniss is assigned to advances further into the Capitol, so the meaning of the revolution is slowly revealed. What do we find as we reach the center of the Capitol, and the heart of the revolution?

At the climax of the trilogy, having survived two battles to the death and become a pawn in a power struggle that could wipe out the people of Panem, Katniss faces a decision that will shape the future. But the meaning of the ending, and therefore of the series, has largely been overlooked. It's much more radical than is often supposed.

In our world, some sort of revolution may be inevitable. Elites are increasingly emmiserating the middle class, having exploited the working class to the point where little more can be taken from them. But whether the revolution is just, and whether it brings justice, are other questions.

"If you had any delusions about having power, I'd let them go now"

The Hunger Games seems to subvert the typical hero's journey. For most of the time, Katniss is an unknowing participant in the rebellion. In the first part of the story, Katniss is mainly concerned with saving her family, but her inherent compassion has wider political consequences. In the second part of the story, Katniss is focused on saving Peeta, but she becomes a symbol of rebellion. At the end of this second part, it turns out there's a full revolution in progress, engineered by a hidden, highly disciplined cell, and fueled by growing dissent in the most destitute districts.

Katniss had no idea about this rebellion being plotted beyond the scenes. In the third part of the story, she's the figurehead of the rebellion, but only its image; she has no influence beyond what she struggles to negotiate with the revolution's commanders. Her apparent lack of political agency is reinforced by its leaders. They never ask Katniss what she thinks, despite her being intuitively bright, brave and compassionate, and the reason they have an opportunity to seize power at all.

At first, Katniss resists this role. She agrees only because she's trying to save Peeta (who's being held hostage by the Capitol) and because of her personal experience of the cruelty of the regime. On one reading then, Katniss is not politically conscious, she's an accidental and reluctant participant, driven by circumstance and necessity. Even her own description of her role positions her as being outside of the revolution ("I want to help the rebels in any way I can"). To some critics, she symbolizes the political hollowness of the story. But as we know, people have a tendency to underestimate Katniss.

Her seeming lack of agency and disinterest in politics is understandable given her pessimism about the possibility of revolution, concern about the costs of conflict, and lack of trust in the revolutionaries. She's wary of the machinations, and the interests, of any elite-led politics and movements, whether it's the Capitol or District 13. And as we'll see, she has grounds to be.

Throughout the story, across its three parts, Katniss' political agency is never properly recognized or acknowledged by others. In fact, she has great, innate political instincts, not from studying theory but from hard experience and practice, and from a basic core set of values that she tries to hold onto. Katniss may not know as much as others, but she knows enough, more in many ways.

"I'm not going anywhere. I'm going to stay right here and cause all kinds of trouble"

It might be the opposite of what the Capitol wants us to believe (and perhaps the leadership of District 13 too), but disobedience big and small is critical to human progress. As Gaston Bachelard wrote ("Prometheus", *Fragments of a Poetics of Fire*):

> To disobey in order to take action is the byword of all creative spirits. The history of human progress amounts to a series of Promethean acts. But autonomy is also attained in the daily workings of individual lives by means of many small Promethean disobediences, at once clever, well thought out, and patiently pursued, so subtle at times as to avoid punishment entirely. All that remains in such a case is an equivocal, diluted form of guilt. I would say that there is good reason to study the dynamics of disobedience, the spark behind all knowledge.

Katniss is an instinctive anarchist, in two main ways.

Firstly, in the common sense meaning of the word. She's a natural rule-breaker. When we first meet her, she's escaping under the fence surrounding District 12, finding her freedom in the meadow and the woods, however temporarily, hunting illegally to feed her family, and hustling in the Hob.

Then, in a moment of true character, she sacrifices her life for her sister. She knows she has no chance in the Games, but she won't let the Capitol take the person she cares most about in the world. In the Games themselves, contrary to her own pessimism and against the odds, she retains her integrity and reveals her compassion. She disrupts the Capitol's designs.

Katniss stays true to her principles: her natural suspicion of authority, and her resistance to the rationalization of violence and domination, exploitation and spectacle. In the end, she'll be faced with a decision, one she wasn't expecting, but which will confirm who she is and what she stands for. Katniss doesn't break the rules because she likes to. She's an instinctive anarchist because she tries to stay true to her humane values in the moment, because in a world of lies, living the truth is radical.

"And that, my friends, is how a revolution dies"

Secondly, Katniss' political anarchism is revealed in the final twist to the story.

As the rebels close in on President Snow's mansion at the heart of the Capitol, he's assembled a human shield of children. A hovercraft drops what looks like supplies, but the parachutes explode. As medics rush in to help the wounded, more bombs rip into the crowd. Katniss' sister, Prim, is killed.

The horror marks the end of the regime. But Snow, captured by the rebels and facing execution, suggests to Katniss that both of them have been outplayed by Coin, that Coin planned the incident to destroy his remaining support in the Capitol ("I'm afraid we have both been played for fools"). Gale, who helped to design the bombs, may also be implicated in the atrocity.

"Now I will kill him. And then the Hunger Games will be over..."

As promised by the now President Coin, Katniss, dressed one last time in her Mockingjay costume, will get to execute Snow in a public ceremony. But just before the ceremony, Coin calls a meeting of the surviving victors. To satisfy the districts' demand for justice and to avoid an ongoing civil war in which more people would die, Coin proposes a "final, symbolic" Hunger Games involving the children of those who held power in the Capitol. (As Alice Miller would ask, why is it always children who need to be punished for the crimes of adults?)

An appalled Peeta rejects the plan ("This is why we rebelled! Remember?") But a distraught Katniss supports the proposal – for Prim, she says.

"Listen to that. The Mockingjay found her voice"

And so we reach the point Katniss has fought for, dreamed of, in her angriest moments. But instead of executing Snow, Katniss uses her one shot to kill President Coin.

Katniss is an anarchist because she stands against authority, domination and cruelty. Killing Coin is the natural consequence, the necessity, of her desire for all of the power games to come to an end.

From early on in the story, Katniss has had a tendency to focus her anger on individuals rather than the system. She might disdain the Capitol, but she seems much more disgusted by Snow. As she later says in her role as the Mockingjay: "We all have one enemy, and that's President Snow. He corrupts everyone and everything. He turns the best of us against each other. Stop killing for him! Tonight, turn your weapons to the Capitol. Turn your weapons to Snow!"

But by the end of the story, with the suspicion that Coin orchestrated the killing of the Capitol children and her proposal for a final Hunger Games, it's clear that it was never just about Snow, about one ruler. Katniss sees that the problem is power, starting with the idea that people can be sacrificed by authority in the name of "peace."

Katniss knows that killing Coin won't be the end of power,

but it sure makes a statement.

"I'm tired of being a piece in their games"

It's not just that Katniss is weary, exhausted, by war, and sees what conflict has produced: yet another dehumanized, potentially authoritarian response. It's that she recognizes that the revolution represents a further manipulation. It will not end the cruelty and exploitation, not as long as the same Hobbesian values underpin the state, that violence and domination are justified in the name of order.

The revolution exploited her natural integrity and defiance. Through clever propaganda and planning it succeeded in bringing down the Capitol against seemingly impossible odds. It manouvered the Capitol into committing ever greater cruelties until the people of Panem had no choice but to rebel.

But the Mockingjay revolution was never Katniss' revolution. That's something different, something we'll discuss in the next chapter. It's significant that Katniss resisted playing the role of the great savior of the masses, that she was so suspicious of romantic revolutionary politics and the real motives that can lie beneath the mask. For Katniss, embodying anarchism, it's more important to live as if another world is possible now, rather than through violent confrontation with the state.

When some commentators criticize the supposedly "empty politics" of *The Hunger Games* then, they reveal more about themselves than they might think. Their revolution is much less radical than they pretend if it only replaces one set of leaders with another. In contrast, Katniss' continued defiance is not how a revolution dies. It's how it lives.

"This is why no one lets you make the plans"

If Panem and the Capitol represent the future of authoritarian state capitalism, and the revolution the possibility of a dangerous continuation of many of the same values, then Katniss' actions represent an instinctive, anti-authoritarian politics, so natural and relatable that we don't even recognize it as being that radical. But in our world, it really is.

Anarchism is the belief that people, as social creatures, are capable of organizing their affairs in such a way as to include equality and cooperation instead of hierarchy, authority or coercion. It's not an invitation to chaos; on the contrary, it believes that a better social order can (only) come from people being genuinely able to associate freely. As the anarchist Gustav Landauer asserted, "The state is a condition, a certain relationship between human beings, a mode of behavior; we destroy it by contracting other relationships." Which is what Katniss tried to do in the Games of course. Anarchy, the condition in which anarchism is realized, is one in which mutual aid and cooperation replace competition, where plenty replaces contrived scarcity, where connection replaces atomization and alienation, and where compassion replaces conflict.

Anarchism is about revolution, but crucially, about living it now. For anarchists, revolution is a process. We need to bring into being in the present what we desire in the future. The revolution is not some utopian society that we might achieve someday, it's the process of making radical change today.

There is no liberation except for self-liberation. People cannot ultimately be liberated by others, only by themselves. No revolutionary elite, no vanguard, no small group of enlightened intellectuals can free the "masses" on their behalf. The true revolution must be made by people, not for them. The authentic anarchist project is to help people empower and educate themselves.

Mockingjay refutes the idea that we can change a system simply by deposing a despot and replacing him or her with a different leader. Coin ends up echoing Snow; of course she does, because she wants the same power that comes from leading the same state.

Instead, we need to believe that another Panem is possible.

"Let's just go end this thing"

As suggested, the Hunger Games play two primary roles: they model and glorify brutal competitive individualism; and (however ironically) they act as a Hobbesian warning, that this is what life would be like if there was no Capitol, no disciplining father figure punishing people "for their own good." This is also what the Treaty of Treason is: an "offer" of basic security in exchange for order, submission, servility. But for anarchists, it's the state that's the real source of war and violence. We've seen this all along: in the Games themselves of course, the promotion of violent competition, the repression of the Peacekeepers, the division of the districts and their extreme exploitation by the Capitol.

But there's the revolution as well. For example, although Gale thinks he's on Katniss' side, she realizes that he's perpetuating the larger problem, the problem of war itself. Snow's regime is a particularly horrific version of a militaristic society, but there can easily be others. What Katniss is trying to overthrow can't just be one regime, it has to be any system founded on power, force and military might, every regime that plays the game of war and conflict.

Katniss does the only thing she can to reject Coin's new regime, including its version of "justice." She knows that a genuinely egalitarian, truly free society can't be built on the back of hierarchy, even a revolutionary hierarchy forged in a time of war. When Katniss kills Coin, it's not that she rejects the revolution or revolutionary politics, rather it's the moment when she becomes a true revolutionary. For the last time in the story, she uses, and subverts, her symbolic power as the Mockingjay. Not to seize Snow's power. To abolish it.

"People of Panem, we fight! We dare to end this hunger for justice"

If *The Hunger Games* was merely "Hollywood Marxism," then it would probably end with Katniss killing Snow, or even more weakly, granting him the justice and mercy that he has denied so many others. Closing the book, or leaving the cinema, we might not notice that the system hasn't really changed.

But that's not how it ends. As Jarrod Shanahan suggests ("The Hunger Games and Revolution", *Jarrod Shanahan*, 27 January 2015):

> [W]hat sets The Hunger Games apart is what made Soviet censors ban one of their country's greatest cinematic achievements: the struggle within the struggle. In *Mockingjay*, Katniss wrestles with the role of mascot for a revolution not controlled by the people but managed from above by an expert class...Katniss knows that an egalitarian society cannot be built using hierarchy, an honest society cannot be built using deceit, and that a revolution willing to sacrifice its very values in the name of victory will be defeated whether it wins or loses. In her dealings with President Coin and the revolutionary leadership of District 13, Katniss comes to recognize that the revolution itself must be the site of struggle, just as much as the society that produced it.

Suzanne Collins may not be an anarchist either, in the proper (political philosophy) meaning of the word. But her story can be best understood as pointing toward a kind of libertarian socialism/anarchism, and the primacy of common humanity, fairness and justice over ideology and power, in the tradition of George Orwell's *Nineteen Eighty-Four* and *Animal Farm* – anti-authoritarian and anti-Stalinist works (as mentioned, the first of these is one of Collins' favorite books).

To Mari Armstrong-Hough, it's a model of total resistance

to power, domination and exploitation: "We see politicking, corruption, and unjustified violence from both the guardians of the status quo in the Capitol and the architects of the rebellion. Katniss, whom we naturally align ourselves with, rejects both these systems." (As quoted in Sarah Seltzer, "Progressive, Tea Party, or Anarchist: Whose Side Is Katniss Really On?", *Flavorwire*, 19 November 2014.)

As Jarrod Shanahan ("The Hunger Games and Revolution") similarly states:

> Katniss' experiences in *Mockingjay* tell us that not only do millions of people know deep down that revolution is the only way out of the present economic, political, and environmental crises, but also that the struggle will be waged not only against capitalism and the state, but against the elements within the revolution which will try to prevent it from going all the way: whether charismatic politicians, self-appointed social movement police, left-talking non-profit organizations, pro-capitalist trade unions, famous Occupiers, or historical re-enacting revolutionary parties.

Katniss' refusal to submit to being the pawn of either the Capitol or District 13 serves as a celebration of, and tribute to, continual resistance.

"He's still playing the game"

Plutarch Heavensbee, formerly the Head Gamemaker and now Director of Communications for the new government, describes the anticipated post-revolution republic as a centralized government with some system of representation. The story, and by implication its author, don't seem too excited about the constitutional republic that the "rebels" plan to establish. Katniss also seems ambivalent, thinking only that "this republic idea sounds like an improvement over our current government."

Given where we are now, let alone where we will be under collapse with its coming authoritarian cruelty and division, if we did manage to rebuild some form of representative democracy, well, there are much worse games to play...

"Do you really know what's going on? And if you don't...find out"

However, there's an even sharper critique of this revolution that Collins includes in her story. What does it mean when it's said that only Heavensbee seems to have won the Games? It's significant that he was both the Gamemaker and a leading architect of the revolution. He bears a Greek name which is linked to dynastic wealth. "Plutocracy" is derived from the Greek word *ploutokratia,* in which *ploutos* means "wealth" and *kratos* means "power" or "rule." This suggests that the revolution, the new republic, won't change the fundamental inequalities in wealth and power of Panem. And it was never meant to.

Plutarch represents the more insightful kind of Capitol insider who looks ahead and sees that at some point the fall of the regime is inevitable. It's just too cruel to survive. But he's personally benefited from the Games and the Capitol, he's risen up to be Head Gamemaker, he's been part of the repression. He doesn't voice disgust at any of it, or express any revolutionary fervor. No, he's the instigator of a revolution designed not to end, but to save the social order, to make Panem safe again for plutocracy.

And given Plutarch's title as head of communications, it suggests that wherever there's a state and rampant inequality there will also be manipulation, distraction and disinformation (he was the one who explained the concept of bread and circuses to Katniss, of course). In this constitutional republic, this new democracy, the game of distracting the populace seems set to continue.

"From what I see here, we've already made history"

The Panemian revolution perhaps most resembles what happened in Romania at the end of the 1980s.

At 12.31pm on December 21, 1989, Nicolae Ceaușescu, the President of Romania, began his address from the balcony of the Central Committee building in Bucharest to the 100,000 people standing below him in Palace Square (now Revolution Square). Just a few minutes later, the mood in the crowd changed. People started to chant "Timișoara," the place where less than a week before the regime had acted against a dissident priest, László Tőkés. Ceaușescu faltered, unsure how to respond. The authorities quickly cut the TV pictures, but the damage was done. The revolution had begun.

That year, communist dictatorships across Eastern and Central Europe had collapsed one after the other. But one leader seemed safe, such was his dominance over "his" country after 42 years of rule. Ceaușescu's was the last remaining communist regime in Europe, and uniquely cruel and corrupt. All key party and state positions were filled by family members or loyal comrades. His wife Elena was deputy prime minister, and his son Nicu was destined to inherit the "throne."

Ceaușescu had developed the largest network of spies in Eastern Europe and silenced all opposition with his secret police force (the Securitate), which had even recruited teenagers and schoolchildren. The regime depended on it. In the early 1980s Ceaușescu had started a program of punishing austerity in an attempt to pay off Romania's national debt, owed to Western banks and accumulated through massive economic mismanagement in the 1970s. Standards of living drastically deteriorated. Ceaușescu ordered the export of much of the country's agricultural and industrial production. Gas, heat and food were rationed. Many Romanians faced malnutrition and the country had the highest infant mortality rate in Europe.

The regime had also banned abortions and contraceptives to

try to keep the population from shrinking, which led to hundreds of thousands of children suffering abuse and neglect in dismal orphanages. The unwanted children were nicknamed "decretei," meaning "children of the decree."

Even so, Romanians couldn't envisage the end of the regime. But a small local protest snowballed into demonstrations and strikes. The authorities reacted with even harsher repression and declared a state of emergency. The public rally in Bucharest was meant to reasert Ceaușescu's popularity, but after dissent spread in the crowd, people fled the square. Troops were mobilized to protect the regime, but by now people were in the streets across the country. Protesters took over the public television building and began broadcasting the revolution live; it was "history's TV revolution." Moments later, Nicolae and Elena Ceaușescu fled the Central Committee building by helicopter. Their escape failed; they were taken into custody by the Securitate, and after a brief "trial," shot to death.

What happened in Romania looked like a classic revolution: there were mass protests, the state responded with violence (more than 1000 people were killed and more than 3000 injured), but the regime crumbled once it was clear it couldn't repress widespread public disgust with its rule. And yet, debate continues to this day about what really took place and whether the revolution was real.

"Real or not real?"

The Romanian revolution appears to have been a combination of a spontaneous uprising and a palace coup d'état against Ceaușescu organized by disaffected parts of the regime. Figures such as Ion Iliescu were presented on television as agents of the revolution, even though they'd had important roles in the ruling communist party. The popular uprising was undirected; it had no strategy or leadership, but it offered the perfect opportunity for the regime's insiders who wanted to seize power as it collapsed.

The structures of the regime were quickly dissolved. The National Salvation Front (NSF) Council was formed to guide the country and organize free elections. But there was confusion; acts of terror by unknown forces, blamed on "foreign terrorists," were taking place across the country. Were some of them orchestrated by the conspirators to create a climate of fear and legitimize their power?

Soon, differences split the NSF. Those who favored the removal of former communists from positions of power and the introduction of reforms left the group; those who remained, the majority of them the former communists, transformed it into a political party with little enthusiasm for real change. Iliescu was appointed president and power remained in the hands of key figures from the old regime. In the 1990 election, Iliescu won 85 percent of the vote and later served two more terms as president.

Much about the revolution remains unknown. Subsequent governments have done little to investigate what really happened and have refused to release key documents relating to it. For many Romanians, communism didn't die with the revolution or the execution of its dictator, it merely put on a new mask. Many members of the former communist elite and security services became extremely wealthy. In 2019, prosecutors accused Iliescu of manipulation and misinformation in the revolution to usurp power. Even today, hardly anyone has been found guilty of even the smallest role in the communist party's half-century reign of terror and misery. Many Romanians live in poverty, especially in rural areas; millions of others, particularly young people, have left the country in search of a better life.

Other revolutions have been accused of being fake. It's also a favorite ploy of authoritarian leaders to claim that "foreign powers" are meddling in their countries and that home-grown protest movements are the puppets of shadowy forces. Which, unfortunately, can sometimes sound more plausible than it should, given that Western governments have historically intervened in many countries – usually not against authoritarian leaders, however, more often against democratically-elected governments that genuinely want to improve the lives of their people.

But as we'll see, whatever the truth of any historical cases, whichever revolutions are deemed real or not by mainstream commentators, this ignores the myriad of struggles that are ongoing around the world, genuine grassroots struggles of resistance which continue to challenge power in all its forms.

"Plutarch doesn't care who dies. Not as long as his Games are a success"

Following the fall of the Capitol, even Plutarch expresses doubts about how long the new reforms will last ("...collective thinking is usually short-lived. We're fickle, stupid beings with short memories and a great gift for self-destruction"). But he adds a hopeful note that this time Panem's political prospects might be different: "Maybe we are witnessing the evolution of the human race."

This sounds hopeful. And yet, read it again. He's really expressing the same pessimistic statist-conservative Hobbesian perspective that led to Panem in the first place. The implication here is that Plutarch suspects, at some point in the future when collective thinking has faded, that more authoritarian measures might once again be required to control our gift for self-destruction.

There's another view, however, that it's the state, power and elite's greed and desire for control that's the problem. If we're in need of evolution, that's where it's really needed.

"Don't trust them. Don't go back"

The Mockingjay was just a projection, that's all it ever was. We're shown as much in the story. Katniss is continually given the scripts to speak, her image is carefully cultivated, her costume created to give an elite-led revolt a credibility it otherwise wouldn't have possessed. It's not the reality of the revolution, just the means to achieve it, to inspire a class consciousness among the downtrodden but divided of the districts, but then to divert it into a palace coup. They're clever, these elites.

The clue was there in the name, taken from an uexpected species, a genetically altered bird with the ability to remember and mimic sounds and share them widely, a symbol of the Capitol's fallibility.

But the real revolution that Katniss represents still lies hidden at the heart of *The Hunger Games*.

Chapter 9

"No Games, no Capitol"

"Slowly, with many lost days, I come back to life"

After killing President Coin, Katniss is tried and acquitted by reason of insanity. She's sent into exile, back to District 12.

The books' ending is more ambiguous than the film. A new government has been established. Katniss returns to the recovering ruins of her old district. She's no longer at risk or hungry, but she is traumatized and anxious about the future.

But over time she begins to heal. There are some things we might never be able to fully recover from, things that will always be with us, but we can learn to function again, even, eventually, to live.

Some commentators suggest the ending is essentially anti-political. Katniss seems to define happiness only in personal, individual terms. She resents that she's been a tool of the revolution: "I was a piece...[u]sed without consent, without knowledge." The new Panem is no utopia. In the longer-term it may not even survive as a free and fair society. Withdrawing from it, at least from its political life, not continuing to fight for justice, isn't this what the Capitol would have wanted? What kind of journey has Katniss been on, if she ends up here?

But there's another interpretation. Katniss not only survived the Hunger Games, she did it through collaboration and compassion. And ultimately, faced with a difficult choice, she stood against hierarchy and exploitation in all its forms, and paid the price. Now, understandably, she hopes for healing. But what many might see as private concerns are actually public and political. They're about how, after conflict and collapse, we might be able to build a new world.

"Did you find what you were looking for?"

Katniss wants to live, beyond oppression and conflict, in peace and security.

The Hunger Games has examined the cost of war, violence and exploitation in personal terms: Katniss' depression and self-doubt, choosing suicide as a way out, her recurring nightmares from the Games, the traumas of the tributes, multiple characters needing to be sedated, Peeta being driven mad...

The ending emphasizes this is not a love story. It's a commentary on capitalism, class and corruption. It's also a warning about where ideologies of domination and control are leading us, and what we'll need to do to survive. Not just survive, but with our inherent human – humane – values intact. It ends about as happily ever after as anything involving children being forced to kill each other can.

When Katniss seems to be struggling to choose between Peeta and Gale (the most likely outcome is that she'll choose neither), there are obviously some romantic feelings involved, but this isn't the core of what her struggle is about. It's about survival with integrity, keeping the true self alive in spite of the deception and brutality all around her. It's about what kind of hope Katniss can allow herself to have, and what kind of future she thinks she deserves.

Katniss giving herself permission to care and be committed to someone (to "owe" them) is political as well. It's about being able to invest in the world, that it's worth doing because there's the possibility of a future beyond mere survival, something that Katniss protects herself from at the start of the story.

Katniss isn't struggling to decide who she loves, she's struggling with whether there could be a place in her life for something as hopeful as love. Because in her world, the Capitol had seemingly crushed all possibility of trust, mutuality, connection, let alone love.

She chooses Peeta, the boy with the bread, who stands for

empathy, self-expression, creativity and compassion. Peeta, who represents a needed different vision of masculinity, beyond violence and domination, rage and entitlement, and toward peace and healing.

"Our future starts tomorrow at dawn"

Still, does the story reflect an empty anti-statism, and ultimately an anti-politics? Katniss may be brave in resisting cruelty and exploitation, but she doesn't seem to have any kind of worked out philosophy, nor express any kind of vision for Panem after the fall of the Capitol. Her "utopia" seems more like freedom from it all.

But maybe that's a good thing. The new Panem remains open, unrealized. Tom Moylan (*Demand the Impossible: Science Fiction and the Utopian Imagination*) used the term "critical utopias" for imperfect places but which have possibility within them:

> A central concern in the critical utopia is the awareness of the limitations of the utopian tradition, so that these texts reject utopia as a blueprint while preserving it as dream. Furthermore, [critical utopian] novels dwell on the conflict between the originary world and the utopian society opposed to it so that the process of social change is more directly articulated. Finally, [they] focus on the continuing presence of difference and imperfection within utopian society itself and thus render more recognizable and dynamic alternatives.

The post-Capitol Panem sketched briefly in *The Hunger Games* could be a critical utopia. Katniss doesn't have a plan, she never really did, but that's the point. She's embodied the values that the old Panem tried to crush, and that the new Panem needs. After all, as Marx wrote (*The German Ideology*): "Communism is for us not a state to be created, nor an ideal to which reality will have to adjust. We call communism the real movement which abolishes the present state. The conditions of this movement result from the premises now in existence."

We don't know what a future without domination and exploitation will look like. But we can still work for it, struggle for it, try to live it. As Alice Miller suggested, we can't know what the world might be like if children were to grow up without being subjected to humiliation, if parents respected them and took them seriously as people. It's worth finding out though. It's not about some perfect theoretical model that must be adhered to. It's about being led by humane values – compassion, mutuality, cooperation, trust – and the kind of society we might build, post-capitalism, post-collapse, that reflects those values.

It's a new day.

"I do not want to lose the boy with the bread"

Suzanne Collins has talked about why she made Peeta a baker, about bread being a main food source in the districts and how it could be the difference between life and death in the Games. As Collins said, "It seemed in keeping with his character to be a baker, a life giver."

Peeta giving Katniss the bread challenges her state of mind. In her desparate desire to survive, she assumes there's no room for the kind of simple, selfless kindness that Peeta showed her in that moment. That's why at first Katniss understands it as somehow transactional, something she needs to pay Peeta back for.

Of course, Katniss is actually a kind person. What she struggles to see in Peeta in that moment is her true self, the one buried beneath all the scars and trauma and struggle to survive. That's why her choice of Peeta at the end of the story isn't for one boy over another, it's for herself, a long denied recognition of her actual qualities and character.

In our world, it's about living beyond capitalism's propaganda and disinformation about ourselves and other people ("Real, or not real?"), and from that, what kind of society might be possible.

"It takes ten times as long to put yourself back together as it does to fall apart"

Further, Katniss' determination to heal and to raise a family isn't an abdication of female power. It's an active, radical, powerful choice. She's choosing peace, to end her participation in the war, to live beyond it. The revolution needs to start with healing and growth.

That's not just individual, it's also about rediscovering collective culture. The maligned people of districts like Appalachia have been the source of some of the country's most important music and culture. But when we first meet her in a future, fascist-dominated Appalachia, Katniss is numb to music, nonplussed about something so seemingly nonessential in her grim world.

Later, in *Mockingjay*, a wedding uses music and dancing from her district. Some of the wealthier districts don't seem to have much culture of their own, closer as they are to the empty consumer hedonism of the Capitol. Katniss allows herself to reflect on the Hanging Tree, a song she remembers from her youth. We realize that she did once have a connection with music, when her father was still alive, before she was consumed by grief and staying alive.

"Rue, who when you ask her what she loves most in the world, replies, of all things, 'Music'"

As Alice Miller put it (*The Drama of the Gifted Child*):

> The true opposite of depression is neither gaiety nor absence of pain, but vitality – the freedom to experience spontaneous feelings. It is part of the kaleidoscope of life that these feelings are not only happy, beautiful, or good but can reflect the entire range of human experience, including envy, jealousy,

rage, disgust, greed, despair, and grief. But this freedom cannot be achieved if its childhood roots are cut off.

Katniss was dismissive of music not because it's useless, but because she needed to cut herself off from the feelings it can generate. She may have regularly escaped under the fence surrounding District 12, but she'd imprisoned herself more than the Capitol ever could.

Writing about the consolations offered by religion, Marx (*A Contribution to the Critique of Hegel's Philosophy of Right*) wrote that: "Criticism has plucked the imaginary flowers on the chain not in order that man shall continue to bear that chain without fantasy or consolation, but so that he shall throw off the chain and pluck the living flower." As Erich Fromm (*On Being Human*) put it, here Marx "conveys the idea that the aim of life is not the drabness of making a living but the beauty of being. To Marx, in a socialist society, when man has become fully himself, there is no need for religion, because the flowering quality of life will be expressed in the whole of daily life and not in a separate and necessarily alienated sector of life..." No need for any other illusions either.

Today, we often regard many other phenomena as acting as opiates: television, popular entertainment, social media, celebrity, fandom, sports...The Capitol's Games represent a fascistic fusion of all of these. But the story suggests that, ultimately, this doesn't work. People want the truth of this world, so that they may finally experience flourishing in the entirety of their existence. They want the living flower.

"I begin to sing"

Not every distraction is a distraction. Some are necessary to feel alive. There is an alternative to the bread and circuses of the Capitol. It's the bread and roses we claim for being alive.

"Bread and roses" is a political slogan, and the name of a

poem and song. It's associated with the successful textile strike in Lawrence, Massachusetts in 1912, now known as the Bread and Roses strike. This, the first large-scale industrial strike in the United States, is one of the most inspiring episodes of working-class history.

Massachusetts had passed a law reducing the working week for women and children from 56 to 54 hours. The mill owners responded by cutting pay; some workers took home as little as $6 a week. The workers responded by striking. Hundreds, thousands, then tens of thousands of textile workers walked off the job. They were largely immigrants, women and children, originating from 50 countries and speaking more than 20 languages.

The strikers' endurance during the freezing winter surprised the mill owners, who assumed that their diversity would keep them from organizing effectively. The more conservative labor unions were equally pessimistic. But the strikers received help from the Industrial Workers of the World (the Wobblies), who planned marches and helped to raise money.

At one point, to keep them safe, the strikers' children were sent away to stay with relatives, but the authorities tried to stop them from leaving. Mothers trying to get their children onto trains were beaten by the police. This prompted a congressional investigation in which children testified about the deplorable working conditions in the mills.

Two years before the strike, in June 1910, an automobile campaign had been organized around the state of Illinois for the right of women to vote. Helen Todd was a factory inspector who represented women and called for laws concerning wages, working hours and conditions. Todd used the phrase "bread for all, and roses too" in a speech as part of the campaign; it later inspired the poem *Bread and Roses* by James Oppenheim, published in *The American* magazine in December 1911.

Bread and roses refers to the idea that a political movement whose demands are merely material suffers from a poverty of imagination, that survival is not enough. As Todd put it, the bread is home, shelter and security, but the roses are music, education, nature and books. (The logo for the Democratic Socialists of America was also inspired by the slogan.)

In his essay *The Fire Next Time,* James Baldwin says, "To be sensual, I think, is to respect and rejoice in the force of life, of life itself, and to be present in all that one does, from the effort of loving to the breaking of bread...Something very sinister happens to the people of a country when they begin to distrust their own reactions as deeply as they do here [in America], and become as joyless as they have become."

"At this point, unity is essential for our survival"

There was always an alternative to capitolism's Hobbesian order based on fear and obedience. It's solidarity, and contrary to Capitol propaganda, it's entirely natural to us.

As Astra Taylor and Lean Hunt-Hendrix note ("One for All", *New Republic,* 26 August 2019), as a social theory, this idea first emerged in the legal texts of the Roman Empire, although of course as a social practice it goes back long before that; it's how we've survived as a species. In the Roman era, when people held a debt in common they were said to hold it *in solidum.* Being in communal debt was the basis of solidarity, a very different kind of debt to capitalist hierarchical debt. If one individual faltered, its members would either bail each other out or default together.

In its original formulation, solidarity was a common identity underpinned by collective indebtedness and obligation, shared responsibility and risk, interdependence and mutual aid. Terms like "bonds," "trust" and "mutual funds" are now used by bankers to describe financial mechanisms. But real solidarity, in contrast to modern contracts, has to be cultivated. It's the practice of creating social ties, of inventing collective identity.

In the early nineteenth century, solidarity became central to the growing labor movement. Craftsmen and laborers from a range of industries, who once saw themselves as unconnected, began to share a larger common character as workers. As industrialization spread, this new working class strengthened their common bonds through acts of resistance and strikes. Solidarity was also central to the creation of welfare systems and social safety nets.

These understandings of social belonging have been eroded under the corrosive pressures of contemporary life. Modernity made the individual sacred, but also separated, isolated, as we saw in the statistics on mental health. Capitol propaganda and division has also de-socialized us, through economic stratification, privileges for some, and shaming the poor.

Today, "solidarity" is most associated with inter-group expressions of comradeship, for example international campaigns in support of groups resisting oppression. Such campaigns say we do not agree, we do not condone. (As noted in the prologue, solidarity is also crucial to direct action movements, as in the Hong Kong protests.) Perhaps, in place of nationalistic supposedly unifying myths, we might be able to tell alternative stories, including for democratic self-governance at a global level. To Hauke Brunkhorst (*Solidarity: From Civic Friendship to a Global Legal Community*), this might be being modeled in recent global protest movements, the beginning perhaps of a transnational civic solidarity.

The enormous challenges we face, from capitalist authoritarianism to climate change, require that social movements forge a radical solidarity. Building of bonds and diverse coalitions is essential to the struggle for a just world. The Capitol will of course push back, buying off some of us, but mostly trying to turn us on each other, to keep their games going. But there is no survival, let alone freedom, without each other.

"Now you're talking"

Katniss seems unconvinced by Plutarch Heavensbee's republic. Her skepticism is well-founded. Not from a Hobbesian point of view (that we're essentially brutish and evil), but because if we retain the same set of values, a different system of government is unlikely to make much difference.

The same greed, selfishness, desire for power and domination among a minority of people risk leading us back to the same exploitation and authoritarianism. And the same fears, of scarcity and of each other, will leave the rest of us vulnerable to their propaganda and manipulations.

We need a deeper revolution, in values, ethics, peace and anti-authoritarianism. This is why we all require recovery and healing from capitalism/capitolism. Our minds have been hijacked. We've assimilated many of the Capitol's values of competition, power, hierarchy and dominance, often without recognizing it. And from this, it's only a small step to accepting the use of force in realizing these values and to accepting this as natural and normal.

Hobbesianism, capitalism, capitolism, imperialism, classism have gone so deep, the revolution isn't an event, it's a (long) process, one requiring "evolution." A change of regime isn't the end of it.

We've been asking the wrong question then. It's not how might the revolution come about, but how it could be a real revolution, how we could come home to our innate values of equality, fraternity, cooperation and mutuality.

"I should have tried to save you"

Katniss doesn't follow Peeta's advice, that killing Snow would make the war worthwhile, meaningful. Or rather, she chooses to target a more urgent threat, the risk of one authoritarian regime replacing another. But what he says raises the question of how to find meaning and resolution after war and conflict, how to hold those who are complicit to account, but at the same time establish justice and fairness.

This tension is played out in the relationship between Katniss and Gale. In *Mockingjay* (the book), Gale questions Katniss' attachment to her former prep (pre-Games preparation) team. Katniss says they're like children who can't be held responsible for the Capitol's cruelty (foreshadowing the choice she will have to make regarding President Coin's proposal for a "final" Hunger Games): "They don't see...I mean, they don't know..." But Gale responds, "They don't know what, Katniss? That tributes...are forced to fight to the death?...Was that a big secret in the Capitol?" Katniss awkwardly replies that the residents of the Capitol were raised on it, it was normal for them.

Perhaps Katniss is also thinking about her own former complicity. In the first book, on the eve of the Games, Katniss and Peeta go to the roof of the Capitol building where the tributes train, where they can speak without being overheard (there's an electrified field around it so that the tributes can't jump to their deaths, foreshadowing the ending of the 74th Games). Katniss recalls that she and Gale were hunting in the woods one day when they saw a ragged-looking girl and boy running in terror. A Capitol hovercraft appeared and captured the girl in a net. It hauled her up, and shot the boy through with a spear. Then the hovercraft disappeared. Katniss says for a moment, before the girl was taken, she locked eyes with her, but did nothing to try to save her. The memory still haunts her.

Katniss comes face-to-face with the girl again in the Capitol – as an Avox, a person who's committed some "crime" against the Capitol and has had their tongue cut out so they can't speak. It's a grim irony: Katniss failed to stand up for the girl ("Just like I was watching the Games"), but it's the girl who's permanently silenced.

In the end, Katniss' decision suggests that she recognizes that killing Snow wouldn't provide meaning to the lives that have been lost. What would is living in a world that doesn't justify destroying lives in the name of "justice," that there's no peace in any state that does.

This is a question many countries have faced of course. A desire for retribution might be understandable, but it can corrupt as well. It won't do the work of healing, justice and peace.

"But to be honest, I'm not the forgiving type"

In his *Principles of Social Reconstruction* (published in 1916, originally titled *Why Men Fight*), the philosopher and peace campaigner Bertrand Russell proposed a more fundamental approach, focusing on changing the values that lead to war and conflict in the first place.

Russell argued that after the experience of the First World War, the individualism had reached its limits. Political theory should be based on creativity rather than on competition: "The supreme principle, both in politics and in private life, should be to promote all that is creative, and so to diminish the impulses and desires that center round possession."

Following a violent conflict, social cohesion may be almost nonexistent. Returnees, combatants and victims often have great difficulty finding their place in the community again. Local institutions that helped bind the population before the conflict may lie shattered. Without the tolerance and cohesion that enables peaceful coexistence, individuals and communities could once again resort to violence to address their grievances.

To Russell, social reconstruction is a condition in which the population achieves a level of tolerance and peaceful coexistence, gains social cohesion through acceptance of a national identity that transcends individual and sectarian differences, has the mechanisms and will to resolve disputes nonviolently, and develops institutions that bind society across divisions. It includes twin, related approaches: directly addressing the legacy of violent conflict through inter- and intra-group reconciliation;

and indirectly building social links by promoting reconciliation through community-based development and cooperative action.

Truth telling institutions are critical. One day, we'll live in a post-capitalist/capitolist world. Truth telling will be crucial to social reconstruction, truth about what was done in the name of power and domination, othering and exclusion, and how these "values" were rationalized. This will require all of us to recognize our various complicities with the Capitol.

So, it works both ways. Healing from trauma, and social change, are interdependent. Therapy can be effective in addressing trauma, but in practice it typically focuses solely on the individual, failing to integrate the beliefs, norms, practices and policies that create trauma in the first place (according to Staci K. Haines in *The Politics of Trauma: Somatics, Healing, and Social Justice*).

The same goes for societies. Healing needs to be collective. Following conflict, the public recounting of memories of violence is a common technique for confronting the past. However difficult, truth telling is founded on the idea that a comprehensive understanding of conflict can help to restore social health. This has been described as historical justice, often pursued through establishing truth commissions which seek to uncover the past and bring to light the violations that occurred on all sides of the conflict.

Such initiatives aren't described in *The Hunger Games*. There is a mention of memorials to what happened and teaching the real history of Panem in schools. Let's hope there's also a process of reconciliation. Otherwise, as per Plutarch's pessimism, there's the danger of repeating the past.

"I'm with the Mockingjay"

To change, to heal, requires more than just instituting a system of representative democracy. Katniss embodies a more fundamental democracy, of anti-violence, peace, collaboration, cooperation, love. And by implication, a society that is decentralized, demilitarized, de-stratified, de-violenced.

This is Katniss' real journey through *The Hunger Games*, a journey toward anarchism. Katniss has the courage to try to take the simple principles of common decency that we often try to live by and follow them to their logical conclusion, what David Graeber (*Debt: The First 5,000 Years*) calls "baseline communism," "...the raw material of sociality, a recognition of our ultimate interdependence that is the ultimate substance of social peace."

Anarchists desire to abolish all relations that can only be maintained by the threat of force. They believe it's possible to have a society based on principles of self-organization, voluntary association and mutual aid. As described by Graeber, and many others, anarchism is based on a simple but powerful set of core principles, that: power and authority corrupt; liberty is possible and desirable; human beings are as reasonable and decent as they're allowed to be; and they can organize their own communities.

When Katniss shoots the arrow that kills Coin, she's really aiming at the idea of power, that we need a strong central authority to police and punish us.

"I'm not afraid"

Katniss also embodies another core anarchist principle, that of self-questioning of her own actions and motives (although as discussed, this is also partly out of a negative self-image born of the Capitol's shaming). This lasts to the end, for example her questioning about whether to have children, the sense of responsibility she puts on this decision. This isn't about complex political theory, it's about trying to act out the right values and resist the Capitol's hijacking, in each and every moment.

This commitment to truth, even when it's difficult and uncomfortable, especially when it is, also has a crucial political purpose in resisting power and domination. As Alice Miller (*The*

Truth Will Set You Free) argues: "Only if we fear the confrontation with our own histories will we need to have power over others and cling to it with all our might...In order to tell the truth we do not need to have power over others. Power is something we only need in order to spread lies and hypocrisy, to mouth empty words and pretend they are true."

The Capitol tries to propagandize our supposed state of nature and propensity for (violent) competition. But as Katniss demonstrates, this is all wrong. We need to recognize mutuality and cooperation where it exists around us, and, like Katniss, sometimes act as if it exists where it doesn't in order to bring it into being. Another world is possible right now, by taking direct action to live in that desired world by peaceful means, to create the future we want in the present.

"I was hoping you'd find your way here"

Now, in District 12, there's a medicine factory instead of the mines (medicines that were denied under Capitol rule). Dirty, dangerous and exploitative work has been replaced by something that heals. Farming too. There's no need for the hunger games, because there's no Capitol that needs to starve people into submission. Presumably, the districts trade with each other, making the most of their historic expertise. But in this healing District 12, there's also security in self-sufficiency.

Collins doesn't go into any detail about the economy of the new Panem, but it sounds like there's a decisive move away from the former regimented specialization, and freedom for the districts to determine their own economic futures. It would certainly make sense for the districts to never again want to be subservient in someone else's economy. Perhaps the factories and the farms are community-owned, held in common by the districts, designed to serve the needs of their residents rather than some far-off rapacious elite.

The "small is beautiful" tradition in eco-socialist/libertarian/

anarchist thought has often been derided and dismissed by statist, centralizing socialists. But in addition to providing people with economic dignity, the control and purpose that are core to mental wellbeing, these local structures are crucial to real collective self-determination.

As Rob Hopkins, founder of the Transition Towns movement, puts it:

> Anarchist Emma Goldman referred to a liberated existence as "simpler, but far deeper and richer" – I say that this is the essence of reinhabitation. It is, in the most profound sense, being somewhere. It is shaping and feeding the landbase as the landbase feeds and shapes you, consciously being part of the interconnected senses and metabolic processes of one's ecosystem, coparticipating with other creatures to tend to the whole that sustains us all. Against the globalism of modernity, we assert a return to place.

Hopefully, Panem won't soon forget what brought down the Capitol after so many decades of suffering, what started with Katniss, and that the values that inspired the districts' defiance also inform the country's economic structure: cooperation, mutuality, interdependence. That these values are the soil that nurtures communities to grow into places grounded in compassion and care, security and support, resilience and renewal, creativity and culture. Hopefully.

Katniss is wrong about one thing. Someone has seeded this. She has.

"You can do it. We both can. We're victors, remember? We're the ones who can survive anything they throw at us"

Hope and humanity are what we need to hang onto, our dandelions in the spring, as Katniss puts it. "The bright yellow that means rebirth instead of destruction. The promise that life can go on, no matter how bad our losses."

Remember from earlier in the story, after Peeta gave Katniss the bread that saved her family from starvation, she saw him at school near a field of dandelions. When Katniss sees the field she gains confidence in her ability to feed her family. The dandelion becomes a symbol of hope for Katniss and evidence of her resourcefulness and expert foraging, a way to survive.

Katniss sees that cruelty and neglect are not all there is. She'd learned from her father's book on plants that dandelions could be used for food. In the first book, when Katniss throws the cookies Peeta's father gave to her after the reaping out the window of the train, they fall open next to a bunch of dandelions – a small sign that Katniss had momentarily forgotten the lesson, that hope is always there. She re-learns this in the end.

Incidentally (or perhaps not, given Suzanne Collins' careful selection of imagery), dandelions have often been a maligned plant, historically dismissed as mere weeds. But the dandelion has a double life. It transforms. It bursts from bud to golden glory before curling up again. Then it lets slip its withered outer shawl and emerges dressed in seed-bearing fruit. These wispy white feathers will sail in the breeze to make new roots in the earth.

Dandelions are practical and beautiful. They're survivors.

"We never arrived...but I felt happy"

Katniss makes it to the meadow in the end, no longer having to sneak under the fence or watch out for Peacekeepers. It's freedom, nature, de-fenced, de-privatized, a space to heal and play. The brutal competition designed to discipline the poor is history. Whether the power structure that benefited the corrupt idle rich will return remains to be seen. But for the moment, the people of Panem have demonstrated that power can be defied and demolished.

Katniss is still alive, still nurturing others. For a long time she resists having children. She recognizes how deeply she's been traumatized, and perhaps she doesn't trust the new Panem. But many years later, feeling safer, she becomes a parent, with Peeta. She's found a place, not escaping anymore, not succumbing to brutality despite everything that's happened.

Collins doesn't pretend it's utopia. She's more sensitive to the emotional and psychological lives of her characters than that. But we've made it here: raising a new generation, teaching new values, building peace. In her work, Alice Miller fought against the transfer of feelings of humiliation and powerlessness into the pedgagogy of authoritarian obedience to children, and instead urged the telling and teaching of the truth. This is what Katniss and Peeta, and hopefully the whole of Panem, are doing for their own children, breaking the chain of cruelty.

"The sun persists in rising, so I make myself stand"

We don't learn enough from the brief epilogue included in *Mockingjay*, but perhaps Katniss also recognizes what Alice Miller suggests we really require to heal (*The Body Never Lies*): "The path to adulthood lies not in tolerance for the cruelties we have been exposed to but in the realization of our own truth and the development of empathy for the maltreated child. It lies in the appreciation of the way in which cruelties have handicapped our whole." Katniss needs to discover the empathy for herself that she's demonstrated for others.

We dream of being whole again, to move beyond feeling fragmented, alienated, compartmentalized, contained. This might sound soft, apolitical. But achieving it requires a revolution, against poisonous pedagogy and authoritarian thinking, obedience and calls for "forgiveness." As the Czech writer Milan Kundera put it in *The Book of Laughter and Forgetting*, "the struggle of man against power is the struggle of memory against forgetting." So it is in the new Panem – as long as we don't forget, numb ourselves or hide behind survival rather than striving for really living.

Alice Miller once wrote that (*The Drama of the Gifted Child*), "Where there had been only fearful emptiness or equally frightening grandiose fantasies, an unexpected wealth of vitality is now discovered. This is not a homecoming, since this home has never before existed. It is the creation of home."

It's not utopia. Nowhere is. But there are much worse places to live.

Epilogue: "Here's some advice. Stay alive"

At the beginning of the story, Katniss is deadened, by constantly scraping for survival under an exploitative economic system, by knowing it's not safe to speak her mind under an autocratic regime that relishes punishing its opponents, by the all-pervading cruelty and violence of the Capitol.

Then it gets even worse. She's forced to fight and kill in the brutal arena of the Games, not once but twice. But she finds a way to hold onto her humanity, just about, to defy a vicious, greedy regime by acting with kindness and compassion, and by recognizing that others can act in the same way too.

That's what "stay alive" – Haymitch's seemingly simple advice to her and Peeta before the Games – really means. Not just surviving, though this is critical in collapse. But staying alive psychologically, by preserving our core humanity in compassion and collaboration, and avoiding succumbing to hatred and a fear of others in a world of scarcity. Emotionally, by protecting ourselves against being damaged and desensitized, so that later we can begin to build new and better worlds. Politically, by retaining our critical thinking about power, and constantly questioning whether centralization and hierarchy are necessary. Intellectually, by resisting propaganda and misinformation, and always asking what's really true, what we can see all around us, feel and experience for ourselves. And authentically, by acting in the belief that the revolution starts with you, that you hold its values in your actions today, tomorrow and everyday.

Katniss and Peeta don't know it at the time, but what Haymitch is saying is that staying alive means keeping the revolution alive. And the final meaning of *The Hunger Games* is that truly staying alive, with our innate human attachment to sharing and solidarity intact, is crucial to our collective survival and the only chance we have of building a Panem based on peace and justice.

As James Baldwin reminds us (*Nothing Personal*, with Richard Avedon):

> One must say Yes to life, and embrace it wherever it is found – and it is found in terrible places...For nothing is fixed, forever and forever, it is not fixed; the earth is always shifting, the light is always changing, the sea does not cease to grind down rock. Generations do not cease to be born, and we are responsible to them because we are the only witnesses they have. The sea rises, the light fails, lovers cling to each other and children cling to us. The moment we cease to hold each other, the moment we break faith with one another, the sea engulfs us and the light goes out.

There's hope in young people today. It's the real reason why older commentators deride them for being soft, emotional, irrational. At some level, these commentators know that a new set of values, held in a new generation, is coming to replace them, that their Capitol will crumble and collapse. If they can survive, these new generations could lead a revolution of reimagining, remaking and rebuilding.

Alice Miller wrote that (*Breaking Down the Wall of Silence*):

> Today, we are at a turning point in our history. We can no longer continue to accept tradition for tradition's sake. We can no longer go on playing the same old war games without eventually becoming conscious of the dimensions of the destruction involved. We must realize that child murder was also part of our "traditions" and that our blindness in respect of this tradition is itself a consequence of this practice. We have no other choice but to become fully conscious of the darker aspects of our own cultural heritage. Only then will we cease to pass them blindly on to future generations.

In the end, Suzanne Collins offers a glimpse of peace, beginning, after all the conflict and exploitation, with the reconciliation we need to make with ourselves.

This is the Dandelion Revolution, and it begins with us.

Good luck, girl on fire.

"Thank you for your consideration" (author epilogue)

Thank you for buying *Stay Alive*, and for making it this far.

The subject of my previous book, *Welcome to the Rebellion: A New Hope In Radical Politics* (Zero Books, 2000), was *Star Wars*, except it wasn't really. That book was really about hope in politics.

I never expected to write a book about *Star Wars*, or rather, to use the saga to discuss contemporary politics: the importance of belief in dark times, the value of collective camraderie, the need to stand against empire, and the new spirit of rebellion evident in protest movements led by young people.

As I wrote in that book, while I've never been immersed in every corner of George Lucas' galaxy, I was certainly a fan of the saga when the original trilogy was released. *A New Hope* was the first film I saw at the cinema, and it represented a whole new world: thrilling, funny, scary at times, and optimistic about what a small group of people can do in the face of seemingly overwhelming oppression.

At that age, *Star Wars* spoke to me. *The Hunger Games* didn't, however. It's not that I didn't appreciate the films (I hadn't read the novels until I started working on this book). I did think they were strikingly serious, well-made and acted. But partly it was generational: *Star Wars* was to start with a Generation X phenomenon. Sure, some baby boomers enjoyed it as well, but it was a story made for children, and I was a child.

The Hunger Games was never my story. Like *Star Wars*, though, it was made for young people, today's millennials and then Generation Y, and clearly it spoke to them. I came back to this when I was thinking about writing a new book: what stories today are the equivalent of what *Star Wars* was to me?

If *Star Wars* is about hope, in at least a couple of respects *The*

Hunger Games is about the lack of it. As I note here, its characters are fatalistic about the possibility of changing Panem. And so, it seems, many young people today are pessimistic about how we'll face the crises that are likely to define their world in the twenty-first century. A certain degree of hopelessness is important. It's more dangerous to be naive about what could happen over the next couple of decades or so. The question is, how do we respond, and how can we rebuild after collapse?

This book doesn't provide personal advice. We have to find our own way. But maybe we're not so alone as we sometimes think we are. Maybe together we can get through it. That's what I take from *The Hunger Games*, and, based on its success, many other people do too.

If you have a few moments, please do leave a review (whether you liked the book or not) on the usual book-selling sites. I'd really appreciate it. And if you'd be interested in hearing about forthcoming books, do visit my website at: www.drmichaeljharrisbooks.com

So, thanks again. And as they say, may the odds be ever in your favor.

zer0
books

CULTURE, SOCIETY & POLITICS

The modern world is at an impasse. Disasters scroll across our smartphone screens and we're invited to like, follow or upvote, but critical thinking is harder and harder to find. Rather than connecting us in common struggle and debate, the internet has sped up and deepened a long-standing process of alienation and atomization. Zer0 Books wants to work against this trend.
With critical theory as our jumping off point, we aim to publish books that make our readers uncomfortable. We want to move beyond received opinions.
Zer0 Books is on the left and wants to reinvent the left. We are sick of the injustice, the suffering, and the stupidity that defines both our political and cultural world, and we aim to find a new foundation for a new struggle.

If this book has helped you to clarify an idea, solve a problem or extend your knowledge, you may want to check out our online content as well. Look for Zer0 Books: Advancing Conversations in the iTunes directory and for our Zer0 Books YouTube channel.

Popular videos include:

Žižek and the Double Blackmain

The Intellectual Dark Web is a Bad Sign

Can there be an Anti-SJW Left?

Answering Jordan Peterson on Marxism

Follow us on Facebook at https://www.facebook.com/ZeroBooks and Twitter at https://twitter.com/Zer0Books

Bestsellers from Zer0 Books include:

Give Them An Argument
Logic for the Left
Ben Burgis
Many serious leftists have learned to distrust talk of logic. This is a serious mistake.
Paperback: 978-1-78904-210-8 ebook: 978-1-78904-211-5

Poor but Sexy
Culture Clashes in Europe East and West
Agata Pyzik
How the East stayed East and the West stayed West.
Paperback: 978-1-78099-394-2 ebook: 978-1-78099-395-9

An Anthropology of Nothing in Particular
Martin Demant Frederiksen
A journey into the social lives of meaninglessness.
Paperback: 978-1-78535-699-5 ebook: 978-1-78535-700-8

In the Dust of This Planet

Horror of Philosophy vol. 1

Eugene Thacker

In the first of a series of three books on the Horror of Philosophy, *In the Dust of This Planet* offers the genre of horror as a way of thinking about the unthinkable.

Paperback: 978-1-84694-676-9 ebook: 978-1-78099-010-1

The End of Oulipo?

An Attempt to Exhaust a Movement

Lauren Elkin, Veronica Esposito

Paperback: 978-1-78099-655-4 ebook: 978-1-78099-656-1

Capitalist Realism

Is There No Alternative?

Mark Fisher

An analysis of the ways in which capitalism has presented itself as the only realistic political-economic system.

Paperback: 978-1-84694-317-1 ebook: 978-1-78099-734-6

Rebel Rebel

Chris O'Leary

David Bowie: every single song. Everything you want to know, everything you didn't know.

Paperback: 978-1-78099-244-0 ebook: 978-1-78099-713-1

Kill All Normies

Angela Nagle

Online culture wars from 4chan and Tumblr to Trump.

Paperback: 978-1- 78535-543-1 ebook: 978-1-78535-544-8

Cartographies of the Absolute
Alberto Toscano, Jeff Kinkle
An aesthetics of the economy for the twenty-first century.
Paperback: 978-1-78099-275-4 ebook: 978-1-78279-973-3

Malign Velocities
Accelerationism and Capitalism
Benjamin Noys
Long listed for the Bread and Roses Prize 2015, *Malign Velocities* argues against the need for speed, tracking acceleration as the symptom of the ongoing crises of capitalism.
Paperback: 978-1-78279-300-7 ebook: 978-1-78279-299-4

Meat Market
Female Flesh under Capitalism
Laurie Penny
A feminist dissection of women's bodies as the fleshy fulcrum of capitalist cannibalism, whereby women are both consumers and consumed.
Paperback: 978-1-84694-521-2 ebook: 978-1-84694-782-7

Babbling Corpse
Vaporwave and the Commodification of Ghosts
Grafton Tanner
Paperback: 978-1-78279-759-3 ebook: 978-1-78279-760-9

New Work New Culture
Work we want and a culture that strengthens us
Frithjoff Bergmann
A serious alternative for mankind and the planet.
Paperback: 978-1-78904-064-7 ebook: 978-1-78904-065-4

Romeo and Juliet in Palestine

Teaching Under Occupation

Tom Sperlinger

Life in the West Bank, the nature of pedagogy and the role of a university under occupation.

Paperback: 978-1-78279-637-4 ebook: 978-1-78279-636-7

Ghosts of My Life

Writings on Depression, Hauntology and Lost Futures

Mark Fisher

Paperback: 978-1-78099-226-6 ebook: 978-1-78279-624-4

Sweetening the Pill

or How We Got Hooked on Hormonal Birth Control

Holly Grigg-Spall

Has contraception liberated or oppressed women? *Sweetening the Pill* breaks the silence on the dark side of hormonal contraception.

Paperback: 978-1-78099-607-3 ebook: 978-1-78099-608-0

Why Are We The Good Guys?

Reclaiming Your Mind from the Delusions of Propaganda

David Cromwell

A provocative challenge to the standard ideology that Western power is a benevolent force in the world.

Paperback: 978-1-78099-365-2 ebook: 978-1-78099-366-9

The Writing on the Wall

On the Decomposition of Capitalism and its Critics

Anselm Jappe, Alastair Hemmens

A new approach to the meaning of social emancipation.

Paperback: 978-1-78535-581-3 ebook: 978-1-78535-582-0

Enjoying It

Candy Crush and Capitalism

Alfie Bown

A study of enjoyment and of the enjoyment of studying. Bown asks what enjoyment says about us and what we say about enjoyment, and why.

Paperback: 978-1-78535-155-6 ebook: 978-1-78535-156-3

Color, Facture, Art and Design

Iona Singh

This materialist definition of fine-art develops guidelines for architecture, design, cultural-studies and ultimately social change.

Paperback: 978-1-78099-629-5 ebook: 978-1-78099-630-1

Neglected or Misunderstood

The Radical Feminism of Shulamith Firestone

Victoria Margree

An interrogation of issues surrounding gender, biology, sexuality, work and technology, and the ways in which our imaginations continue to be in thrall to ideologies of maternity and the nuclear family.

Paperback: 978-1-78535-539-4 ebook: 978-1-78535-540-0

How to Dismantle the NHS in 10 Easy Steps (Second Edition)

Youssef El-Gingihy

The story of how your NHS was sold off and why you will have to buy private health insurance soon. A new expanded second edition with chapters on junior doctors' strikes and government blueprints for US-style healthcare.

Paperback: 978-1-78904-178-1 ebook: 978-1-78904-179-8

Digesting Recipes
The Art of Culinary Notation
Susannah Worth
A recipe is an instruction, the imperative tone of the expert, but this constraint can offer its own kind of potential. A recipe need not be a domestic trap but might instead offer escape – something to fantasise about or aspire to.
Paperback: 978-1-78279-860-6 ebook: 978-1-78279-859-0